Eat Me

Eat Me

LOVE, SEX AND THE ART OF EATING

By Alexandra Antonioni

HarperCollins*Entertainment*
An Imprint of HarperCollins*Publishers*

HarperCollins*Entertainment*
An Imprint of HarperCollins*Publishers*
77–85 Fulham Palace Road,
Hammersmith, London W6 8JB

www.harpercollins.co.uk

A Paperback Original 2005
1

A catalogue record for this book
is available from the British Library

ISBN 0 00 720664 X

Set in Linotype Sabon

Printed and bound in Italy by
Legoprint Spa

For my family, who have supported me through every *Beginning, Middle* and *End* and without whom my life would be a very empty place indeed.

And for the next generation: James, Max, Cristian and Sacha.

CONTENTS

ACKNOWLEDGEMENTS

I would like to thank all those people who have helped me with this book, especially those who gave me recipes, ideas and real-life stories about their own relationships. Names have been changed to protect the not-so-innocent.

Grazie mille, to my beloved mum and dad, Freddie and Bruna Antonioni, for their overwhelming love and support and for never failing to make me feel like I'm sweet sixteen.

A big thank you to my sister and my favourite brother-in-law (ok, my *only* brother-in-law), Paola and Colin Nutt, who welcomed me into their home and allowed me to scribble away in their basement for weeks at a time, and for always being around to bail me out and check that I'm still breathing. Paola, your boundless enthusiasm for *Eat Me* and the fact that you never failed to laugh at my jokes kept me going. I love you, Sis.

There is no thank you big enough in the whole world for my baby brother, Peter Antonioni. I honestly don't know where I'd be without you, you have made this possible. I O U 1. You're the best friend a girl could have. Gooners forever.

To Sarah Lewis who read the initial draft, believed it *would* get published and then showed it to her dad, Gerald Lewis, who was the first person who made me believe it really *could*.

Thank you also to my friend Paul Harrison – you're full of surprises, one of which was the fortuitous introduction to my agent (I do love saying that!), Peter Burrell, who in turn introduced *Eat Me* to HarperCollins. Peter, you're a superstar as well as being an all-round really good bloke.

And to Marco Pierre White who generously offered to write the foreword, *grazie*, you're a gentleman in the truest sense of the word.

A big, big thank you to Monica Chakraverty at HarperCollins for putting up with all my techno disasters as well as my uncharted forays into the Wild West that is cyberspace; for having the grace to giggle with me when it all went horribly wrong, but especially for being so good at your job and instinctively knowing when something I'd written wasn't quite right. Thanks to you, it is now.

Indeed I'm grateful to everyone at HarperCollins who was involved in this project; it was wonderful to meet you all and I look forward to seeing you for the next one.

Finally, and most importantly, my everlasting gratitude and big love go to Roger Griffith whose unwavering belief in *Eat Me* dragged me kicking and screaming back to the keyboard. But for you this book would have never seen the light of day, your faith in me is humbling. Thank you for this and for so much more. Now if we can just get rid of your obsession with Spurs . . .

FOREWORD

By Marco Pierre White

Quite simply the joy of *Eat Me* is that it extols the virtues of Love, Sex and Food, three things everyone has experience of, and that people just love talking about.

Food has, throughout the ages, been synonymous with hedonistic pleasure, with finding love, falling in love and sometimes losing love. *Eat Me* demonstrates with an informed, seductive and cheeky approach how to marry food with the various stages of romantic relationships. Nothing is left to chance, from first date dinners, post-coital snacks, meeting the future in-laws and making up after your first big row, right through to fabulous recipes for comfort food should it all go horribly wrong. I've been there and I'm quite sure you have too.

Nothing inspires romance quite like food. The cunningly pre-meditated but seemingly effortless way that Alex recommends the seduction and subsequent nurturing of a lover through cooking just can't fail. She uses her kitchen in much the same way a spider uses her web.

Her reminiscences of first-date disasters during supposedly romantic dinners as well as her mischievous take on the nuances of relationships had me roaring with laughter as I recalled some equally excruciating but, with hindsight, bittersweet encounters from my own past.

Along with great menus and some truly honest relationship advice there are moments of déjà vu for us all as we smirk knowingly at some of the insights into the ongoing battle of sexes. To quote a line from *Eat Me:* 'Men are from Earth, Women are from Earth. Deal with it'.

Have fun with *Eat Me*. Open a bottle of wine, put some music on, get into the kitchen and start connecting with the culinary siren you have within. Be spiritually and emotionally nourished, and most of all enjoy.

Marco Pierre White
May 2005

INTRODUCTION

Prior to starting our journey through the mesmerising alchemy that stems from the marriage of food and love, I should like to give you a little background information about myself. So here are a few pertinent details about where I've been and what I've done, which should afford you a better understanding of the author, my credentials and the experiences that have led me to write this book.

I was born in London to Italian parents sometime in the early- to mid-sixties. (I don't like to be too precise about my age, female prerogative and all that, let's just say that I've been around long enough to have learnt about the harsh realities of life, but not so long that I am no longer able to be excited, amazed and enraptured by it.)

Given that my parents owned a restaurant, the Bongusto (which as kids we re-christened the Gone Busto, naturally out of earshot of my father), I was steeped in a foodie culture from a very young age. I have warm and vivid memories of 'going down the shop', as we used to call it, to help out in the school holidays. It was not unusual for there to be three generations of Antonionis in attendance at any one time: my parents, occasionally my grandfather (although he came to eat and generally observe proudly from the sidelines) and we three kids – my older sister and baby brother and me.

We were all working towards the same goal: a successful family restaurant serving first-rate, home-cooked Italian food in a cosy, friendly atmosphere, affording the kind of welcome and familiarity that comes from seeing the same faces over and over again. Many of these people became an integral part of our extended family and even today, long after my father has retired, they still have a place in our hearts.

Having spent the better part of the school holidays and weekends working in the Bongusto it was only natural that I should grow up with a leaning towards hospitality as a career. Having learnt the basics I spread my wings, and in the early Eighties, newly married at the tender age of 20, I moved to Hong Kong with my husband. There I lived and worked for many years managing some truly fabulous restaurants, amongst which was Grissini at the Grand Hyatt Hotel, the brand new and utterly gorgeous diamond in the Grand Hyatt crown.

Grissini was a world away from the Bongusto and, unbeknownst to the hierarchy of Swiss hoteliers that employed me, I was totally inexperienced in the running of a fine dining restaurant. To say that I talked up the family business and my hospitality experience is an understatement – it was a far cry from the family-run, all-day-breakfast café/restaurant of my youth and an extremely steep learning curve. But learn I did; the young, gifted Italian chef at Grissini was a genius and through this book I hope to do him justice in passing on his knowledge of food and its ability to seduce.

Grissini was a highly romantic restaurant in a wonderful setting overlooking Hong Kong harbour; floor-to-ceiling windows afforded fabulous views of the South China Sea. It was a heady time indeed for little Alex Antonioni from North London, to suddenly be presiding over such an exalted dining room full to the rafters with the beautiful people: witnessing their romantic assignations; first dates, reunions, proposals, celebrations, secret trysts and, of course, the occasional tearful parting.

I watched and learned.

It is a fact that every night in a restaurant, any restaurant anywhere in the world, a theatre production takes place: the guests are the star characters and the staff and food their producers and props. Every night there was drama, every night a new lesson in love and life.

Unfortunately, my marriage was not to last and after my divorce I left Hong Kong and returned to London. After a period of settling in, the advent of a fabulous new career in restaurant PR and being very much a single girl about town, I 'serially monogomised' for the first time in my life, enjoying a succession of very agreeable one- to two-year relationships.

Despite the fact that the guys I became involved with turned out to be Mr Right Now rather than Mr Right and the liaisons came to their own natural conclusion, I wouldn't have changed a single thing. I loved, laughed and learned a lot; there is a lot to be said for being an independent, single, successful, commitment-shy woman. The world was now my oyster.

I left for Singapore in the late Nineties where I worked for a couple of years writing restaurant reviews for a local newspaper. After a while the gypsy in my soul needed a change of pace (can you see a pattern forming here?), so, in a bid to reflect on my life and 'find myself', I headed for Australia with no job and no idea of what I was going to do once I got there.

It was there, having been totally captivated by the inspirational Australian food culture, that I first had the idea to write a book incorporating the two things that were so pivotal in my life: Love and Food. I wanted to convey to women how easy it was to seduce a man with food in much the same way that a spider uses her web to entrap her prey.

I spent a year researching the shift in attitudes and other people's perspectives of the sometimes cold, hard world of modern-day dating. It would seem that things have changed a lot and, armed with this information and drawing on my, it has to be said extensive, personal experience and a strong belief about the nurturing effect of food on romantic love, *Eat Me* was born.

This book is best described as a tongue-in-cheek, sometimes searingly honest and occasionally painful journey through the highs and lows of a modern-day relationship for serial romantics who adore food. But, if used correctly, *Eat Me* can also help transform even the most inexperienced and reluctant cook into a culinary siren; one who appreciates the importance of enhancing and nurturing relationships through food and the cooking of it.

THE BEGINNING,
THE MIDDLE,
THE END

(*Manners of a Modern Romance*)

I'm not shooting for a successful relationship.
At this point I'm just looking for something that
will prevent me from throwing myself in front of a bus.
I'm keeping my expectations very, very low.
I am just looking for a mammal. That's my bottom line.
And I'm really very flexible on that too.

LUCILLE BALL

So, my fellow modern-day romantic gourmand, if you have bought this book you are one of the many amongst us who appreciate the unbridled joy that is love combined with the pleasure of all things oral.

Love and Food – the ultimate pairing of the senses. What more could a mere mortal ask for . . . ok, maybe a pair of vintage Manolos, but, hey, can you *eat* them?

Welcome, then, to *Eat Me*, where culinary possibility flirts with romantic probability. Exciting, sensual and utterly blissful, a stimulating and deeply fulfilling manner in which to woo and be wooed, *Eat Me* is neither cookbook nor love story but a journey through modern romantic love (on a full stomach) from start to finish.

Yes, yes already, I know, I said finish.

Before we start on this journey, it is my duty to explain to you the three stages of Love in the game that is modern-day dating.

Think *Bridget Jones*, *Sex and the City*, *9½ Weeks* (the fridge scene!).

Time to wake up and smell the testosterone. Baby, times they are a-changing. Our generation is dealing with a completely different set of rules, which we are playing by ear and making up as we go along. The days of 'Forsaking All Others Forever and Ever, Amen' are but a cloud of well-trodden, soggy confetti in the fairytale nuptials of our wildest imaginations. Divorce is on the up; true love is proving to be more elusive than ever. It is a bona fide serial-dating, bed-hopping jungle out there.

Deal with it.

We live in a world of serial, but temporary, monogamy; a smorgasbord of endless possibility, where a broken heart is no longer terminal but instead easily and endlessly restorable. It happens the moment yet another cutie with the right combination of looks, style and, if we are lucky, cash, appears. He/she will have that certain something, that *je ne sais quoi* that enables him/her to turn our heads and make our bruised and battered little hearts beat, to the sound of *their* drum, that little bit faster.

Hey presto! We are no longer heartbroken, actually we are the opposite: heartsick, horny and in lust. In fact, off, once again, with the fairies.

Today we seek not so much Mr Right as Mr Right Now, thus a staggering percentage of relationships exist in the sphere that is:

'The Beginning' 'The Middle' ' The End'

Hey, back off! I didn't write the rules, so don't shoot the messenger.

Come on, don't get too disheartened, of course True Love exists. Look around you, surely you know loads of people in successful relationships, happily married with a couple of kids, white picket fence, roses over the door, etc? Whaddaya mean they're all divorced? There is no place in our world for such blatant (though, some would say, justified) cynicism. I as the author reserve the right to keep an open mind. One day my prince *will* come, as will yours.

Honest.

Meanwhile, in the parallel universe that is Serial Monogamy, I will embark on every new relationship with relish and have myself an absolute ball. Life is too short to mope around and beat one's, hopefully ample, breast over yet another lost love. Not all men are bastards, just as all women are not gold-digging ball-breakers: this is but an urban myth. I hope.

So there you have it, in most cases life is *not* the fairy-tale we were told it was going to be but, hey, neither is it so bad. We may have to kiss a lot of toads before we find our prince but . . . kissing the right toads, in the right places, whilst feasting on the perfect morsel, can actually be a lot of fun.

Please enjoy your Serial Monogamy in the knowledge that one day, when you are old and grey, rocking in your chair surrounded by your gloriously doting grandchildren (or you're the oldest swinger in town, suckin' down a Margarita with your latest toy boy/girl), you won't regret the things you did.

Only the things you didn't.

> *Your words are my food, your breath my wine,*
> *you are everything to me.*
>
> SARAH BERNHARDT

Right, I'm glad that's over with. Now let's have some fun. Let's talk food, my next favourite subject.

It is my belief that food plays a significant role in the seduction, the pleasuring and the binding together of two newly-dating individuals. This first became apparent when, at the tender age of 16 and a total innocent, I was taken out to dinner on a proper date for the first time ever. Mitch was 24 years old and a friend of a friend, he used to come over to my house and we'd spend hours listening to music and just hanging out. When he asked me to go to dinner I was over the moon, but my parents less so and only allowed me to go out with this ostensibly much older man on the condition that I was home by 11pm, *sharp*.

He picked me up at 7.30pm in his rather flash and very red sports car and took me, at somewhat high speed, to a very 'in' bistro in Mayfair. Walking into that jewelled, cave-like restaurant was the most amazing moment of my thus far rather sheltered 16-year-old life. Everywhere I looked there was glamour, I felt like I'd arrived. As a family we'd always gone to lovely restaurants but this was different, this was very grown up, utterly sophisticated and terribly sexy.

We were seated at a corner table with a bottle of Veuve Clicquot, aka The Widow, which to this day remains my absolute favourite champagne. He ordered for both of us. (So manly.) We started with huge pink prawns dripping with butter and oozing garlic, which we ate with our fingers, catching the butter with our tongues as it dripped.

That was the precise moment that little Alex Antonioni realised that food was sexy. Really, really sexy. My mother had made this same dish a thousand times and it had never had quite this effect on me. This was indeed a revelation.

The prawns were followed by a perfect roast chicken whose ancestry lay in Bresse, France. It was presented to us on a silver salver; a whole roast chicken, crispy and golden and surrounded by perfectly turned baby carrots, tiny little roast potatoes and bunches of watercress to mop up the juices. An impossibly well-dressed waiter carved it in front of us at the table whilst all the other diners looked on enviously. Apparently you had to order this particular dish 48 hours in advance, Mitch had done just that.

I felt like a princess.

Pudding was Crêpes Suzette, which involved more tableside theatricals. Although by this point I think the waiter was just showing off, it was glorious. Piping-hot sticky crêpes were served whilst on fire and to a 16 year-old on a first date it was the absolute height of elegance. I felt like Audrey Hepburn somewhere between *Breakfast at Tiffany's* and *Pygmalion*.

The memory of that meal has remained with me always. Over the course of that evening Mitch, who in reality was just ok-looking, became a prince amongst men. In the flickering candlelight of that restaurant, bewitched by the combination of ice-cold champagne, delicious food and flirtatious, giggly banter, I would have agreed to pretty much anything Mitch had in mind. I was utterly seduced.

My parents knew exactly what they were doing by not letting their daughters out of their sight for too long and when, after another round of coffees and a large Amaretto, I realised to my horror, Cinderella-like, what the time was I somewhat unsteadily left my idyll and Mitch escorted me home.

I was over an hour late. My father's fury, conveyed via a colourful selection of choice words and the slamming of the front door, ensured Mitch never called me again.

Coward!

I never looked at food in quite the same way ever again, hence the concept of *Eat Me*; a collection of anecdotes, suggestions, aphrodisiacs, nibbles, rude food, drinks, dinners, lunches, bed picnics, quotes, feasts, snacks and comfort foods alongside a selection of menus to entertain friends and family that will ensure your lover's full attentions and, well, who knows . . .

THE BEGINNING

There is no sincerer love than the love of food.
GEORGE BERNARD SHAW

Your eyes meet across a crowded room at a party, on the tube, in a pub, at a wedding, down a coalmine, or even at Grandma's funeral. It matters not a jot wheresoever the first glimpse occurs when Cupid's arrow strikes and we meet a stranger who literally, inexplicably, takes our breath away. That spectacular, *bestillmybeatingheart* moment when everyone else in a 5km radius disappears and *kapow*! You are in lust.

Asinine, garbled conversations tend to follow, both stumbling over words, finding everything the other says fascinating, achingly familiar and hysterically funny in equal measure. Then, with slightly glazed eyes and manic grins, numbers are exchanged along with meaningful, longing glances . . . here we go again.

13

THE BEGINNING

The stage is set . . .
The Players are eager to play . . .
Enter stage left, boy meets girl . . .

ATTRACTION

❦

Like a Moth to the Flame

*So, Debbie McGee, what first attracted you
to the millionaire, Paul Daniels?*

MRS MERTON

In order to transform ourselves into the gastro-
nomic goddess we yearn to be it is crucial that we
have a subject, namely a man, around whom we can
weave our culinary magic – and not just any old guy, he
must be someone that we like enough to want to impress
and don our pinny for. If you already have someone in
mind, good for you; for those of us who are still looking,
this chapter is especially for you. (Although, even if you
have your prey in sight don't skip this chapter 'cos, honey,
you never know.)

15

I love to cook and enjoy nothing more than inviting good friends round, cooking up a storm, sharing a few bottles of wine and putting the world to rights. I'm a little more reticent to cook for a man, a new potential Mr Right – I don't flash my copper-bottom pans for just anybody.

The problem is, as I'm getting a little older I'm getting a lot fussier. These days it takes a little more than a cute arse and a moody stare for me to want to grind my spices, rattle those pans and shake my booty.

Much has been written about Attraction. Why is it that some people attract us like a moth to a flame whilst others, for no apparent reason, leave us as cold as yesterday's custard? How is it that one girl's *Titanic* is another girl's *Love Boat*?

I wish I knew. It would certainly facilitate the soul-destroying, life-sapping and ego-wrecking process of trying to meet 'someone new'.

> *Sex appeal is 50 per cent what you've got*
> *and 50 per cent what people think you've got.*

SOPHIA LOREN

From my experience we girls generally go for the same 'type' over and over again, no matter that we *really* should have learnt our lesson by now. With me, it's bad boys. No matter how often it ends in tears I just can't help myself; if they look a little naughty and act a little wild you can be sure I'll be fluttering my eyelashes and simpering in their general direction.

In an attempt at attracting a member of the opposite sex with a view to 'dating', all we can do is make an effort to get out there, put our best foot forward, chest out, tummy in and hope for the best. Or is it? What if we had some pointers? Some inside information?

I asked all the men I knew what they found attractive in women, what it was that caught their eye and captured their hearts. Below, please find the, sometimes unexpected, results of that exhaustive study.

It will come as no surprise to any of us to hear that men fall in love with their eyes and women fall in love with their ears. Guys just cannot help themselves. They are suckers for a pretty face, big boobs, a peach of a bottom and a knowing smile – not necessarily in that order. (Unless they are drunk, in which case they don't care what you look like as long as you agree to go home with them. Tragic, but true. Don't say I didn't warn you.)

However, conversely, are we ladies not in turn attracted to a six-pack? George Clooney? Brad Pitt? And of course, a healthy bank balance always does amazing things to a guy's phwoar-factor. They have their fantasy woman and we have our fantasy guy, but in the real world we don't date the 'fantasy', we date each other.

Are you with me thus far?

Whilst all men (yes, all men, unless of course they're watching football) will do a double take at the sight of a well-stacked babe with a pert bottom, full lips and pelmet skirt, deep down they're not *that* shallow when it comes to choosing a mate for life. They just couldn't be. Could they?

The guys I spoke to inferred that when seeking a Long Term Relationship, the majority of them (did you get that? I said the majority, some are indeed hopeless cases) are not attracted solely to the tits and arse package when it does not include some or all of the following attributes.

Prepare to suspend your deeply cynical beliefs and be amazed.

Beauty came top of the list, although surprisingly men are not as attracted to glamour girls as we think they are. Beauty, it would seem, is indeed in the eye of the beholder.

True, the kind of women they want to date take good care of themselves and of how they look but, apparently, it is not about having the perfect body or looking like the models in the fashion mags (airbrushed within an inch of their skinny, cellulite-free, digitally-enhanced, irritating selves), it is about confidence. If you look good you will feel good, ergo you will be upbeat, friendly and approachable. If you make no effort with yourself, why should anyone make an effort with you?

> *To keep a man you need to be:*
> *a lady in the parlour, a cook in the kitchen*
> *and a whore in the bedroom.*
> JERRY HALL

So it's not about being a perfect '10', it's about being the best you that *you* can possibly be, no matter what you may weigh, how old you are or how much money you have.

Take heart, ladies, here's what men really want, in no particular order:

An infectious giggle, sparkly eyes, manicured hands, a toned body (but definitely not skinny, all the men I spoke to preferred a curvier girl), also important is intelligence and a wicked sense of humour that includes being able to laugh at ourselves.

Men are attracted to women who are independent, have a certain *joie de vivre* and are in control of their own lives. They also like women who are unpredictable, exciting and adventurous, both in and out of the bedroom.

They want a woman with whom they can have fun, who preferably likes football (a tough one I know), who doesn't want to change them (admit it, we've all tried) and who understands when *he's* had a bad day and *he* needs a cuddle.

They are dead keen on women who can cook (funny that), and girls who are not carrying around loads of baggage from past relationships. Having similar interests, ideals and goals is also considered important.

Men adore women who go to dinner and actually *eat*. They want someone who will support them, love their mum and not expect them to give up their mates or spend every Saturday afternoon shopping.

In addition? Men want sex; lots and lots of sex. They never want to hear the words 'Not tonight darling, I have a headache'. Ever.

> *A woman waits motionless until she is wooed.*
> *Much how a spider waits for a fly.*
>
> GEORGE BERNARD SHAW

Ok, now for the gentlemen. What attracts us ladies to men? Good looks are clearly a consideration, but we are not expecting you to look like a movie star. That said, grooming is paramount, we want you to look and smell good. Aftershave should definitely be in evidence, but not so much that we are asphyxiated.

Women have a bit of a thing about men's shoes, my advice is buy the best you can afford and keep 'em polished. Lots of women say a good sense of humour is imperative, make us laugh and it would seem you are home free.

Bottoms came up, a lot. We girls apparently have a bit of a thing for your pert buns, almost as much as we like kind eyes but not as much as we value that old chestnut Good Manners. We like it when men open doors for us, pay for dinner on a first date and talk to our faces rather than our cleavage. We like it when you have orderly, tidy homes and when you listen, really listen, to what we are saying. If we do tell you our problems we don't expect you to fix them, just listen.

Gentlemen, it's better for all concerned that you don't go on and on about football, your bitch/angel/goddess (whichever fits) ex or drone on and on about work. We know you work hard. We do too.

Oh, I nearly forgot, we love that you can cook but please don't do it as well as us.

*Men don't live well by themselves. They don't even
live like people. They live like bears with furniture.*

RUTH RUDNER

Men are having a hard time these days but, conversely, women have never had it so good. (I think.) Apparently we live in an age where Women Can Have It All. But as much as we do want it all, we don't want to lose our femininity and we still want our man to be a real man, even if we are earning more than you and are perfectly capable of changing a fan belt whilst knocking up dinner for ten.

But, and there's always a but, in behaving like the strong, silent, dependable men we yearn for, you must be strong but not too strong. God forbid we should feel patronised or controlled, but there again God help you should you display any sign of weakness. (Understand why I'm feeling a bit sorry for them?)

Gentlemen, we don't want to wear the trousers but we don't want you to wear them either, couldn't we just take a leg each?

Yup, women really can have it all. The job, the kids, the holidays, the money, the perfect relationship, the perfect body, new boobs and smooth botoxed skin that will never age and the most significant validation of all, a trouser leg. It's just that sometimes it's exhausting and we just want a cuddle. And a chocolate biscuit.

> *Intuition is the strange instinct that tells*
> *a woman she's right, whether she is or not.*
>
> OSCAR WILDE

FIRST DATES

First Impressions

Don't think of him as a Date,
Think of him as a Dinner.

LUCILLE BALL

Hopefully our improved talents in the art of attraction will have been put to good use and will have resulted in securing the attentions of an eligible and gorgeous man, one whose sole purpose in life is to ask us out to dinner.

So you've finally got a date, but please don't be tempted to cook, you'll have plenty of time later to wow him with your culinary expertise if the evening goes well. Go out to a lovely restaurant, relax and find out a little more about each other and see if this is worth pursuing.

A propos of not cooking, do take my advice as I'm talking from bitter experience. Every time I have cooked on a first date it has ended in tears, generally mine. Even if the food was perfect and everything looked fabulous, by the time my date arrived I was frizzy-haired and frazzled from the hours spent in the kitchen and from the cleaning regime required to turn my apartment into something out of *Vogue Interiors*.

On one occasion when I was asked out, memorable because I really liked this guy and had been trying to get his attention for months, I decided to dazzle him with both my cooking skills and my fabulous 44th-floor apartment overlooking Hong Kong harbour. So I stupidly (with hindsight) invited him to dinner.

I cleaned, shopped and cooked all day, preparing a menu planned with military precision. Parma ham with Chanterelle melon was followed by an inordinately expensive grilled lobster and a mango soufflé finished off the dinner. The whole meal was washed down with several bottles of Veuve Clicquot. I wore my killer little black dress and lit enough candles to illuminate the Vatican. Everything was perfect.

Except . . . he was Jewish. (Who's to know?) He didn't eat Parma ham (pork) and he didn't eat lobster (shellfish) and hated the perfumed aroma of mangos.

I became increasingly flustered and more than a little resentful that all my hard work had resulted in him nibbling on a breadstick and not much else. Especially not the hostess.

Whilst I'm sure my ill-advised dinner was not solely to blame (I think it was a lot more to do with my evidently increasing displeasure), having eaten the square root of exactly nothing he made his excuses and left. That was the last I heard from him.

Like I said, don't be tempted to cook. (In a fit of pique I ate everything on the table plus all the after-dinner mints so not only did I feel rejected, I also felt fat. Not a good combination.)

Back to happier things.

It doesn't matter how many first dates I've had or how many restaurants I've eaten in, I always get excited about the first time I have dinner with someone new. You never quite know what will happen, there's always the chance that this could be the one.

The problem is, of course, that first dates don't always live up to our expectations. I'm sure we all have a Dating Disasters Dossier, filed away in our memory under Not To Be Repeated Under Any Circumstances. Those dates that forced us to question our apparent inability to spot a really bad idea! How in the name of all that is sacred could we possibly have accepted, or worse yet requested, this interminable torture? I have spent far too many first date dinners surreptitiously glancing at my watch, willing the minutes to tick past whilst seated opposite someone with whom I had absolutely nothing in common and, worse, whom I was starting to actively dislike.

It happens.

Far too bloody often, actually.

You know who you are, guys, those of you from my bleak and beleaguered past that caused me to coin the idiom 'First Date Disorder'. If I looked bored it's because I was. There, now you know.

The tragic thing was that on these ghastly, coma-inducing, sub-standard debacles I invariably ended up paying the bill, purely to prevent any possibility of having to kiss him through some kind of misplaced guilt. Subsequently, I ended up bored to tears, questioning my judgement and, to add insult to injury, considerably poorer.

Oh, the diabolical ignominy!

So, given that all of us must have truly terrible tales of first date disasters why do we repeatedly put ourselves through the lottery-style risk they entail?

That's easy, we just keep going back for more (akin to a boxer who won't stay down), because every now and then we stumble unsuspectingly into first date nirvana, a rare and magical encounter whereby the simple act of having dinner with somebody affords us such exquisite pleasure it erases all memories of the bad dates that have gone before. (I have on occasion experienced this phenomenon and when it's that good, it's the best.)

The problem with these fairytale dates is that I am

unable to eat a single bite during dinner. However, to conceal this angst I have perfected the art of pushing my food round the plate in such as way as to appear to have eaten quite a lot. Later on at home, after an enchanting evening which has me fantasising about our next date – the sexy way he holds his glass and how much I love his voice – I suddenly find that I am starving and heading for the kitchen to make a bacon sandwich!

> *I've had a wonderful evening, but this wasn't it.*
> GROUCHO MARX

What people order on a first date can be a bit of a revelation in terms of their personality and their expectations of the evening ahead. Here are some examples from real dates – this stuff really happened to me. I share it with you so that you can spot the bad bets immediately and not bother with a second date! The female examples, however, I gleaned from my male buddies.

Traits to watch out for when on a first date with a man:

As you sit down he requests a glass of tap water, skips the starter and orders the cheapest main course on the menu, plus a glass of house wine that he nurses all night. He then proceeds to divvy up the bill, ensuring that you pay for the extra coffee you ordered and refusing to pay the service charge.

He's cheap and, worst of all, the man has no style. This is date hell. Dump him.

The first thing he does is order champagne followed by two dozen oysters, he then suggests you skip the main course and have another bottle of fizz instead. He orders a vast dessert meant for two which he spoon-feeds you in a rather suggestive fashion.

This guy wants to get dinner over with as quickly as possible and ply you with enough aphrodisiacs and champagne to guarantee that you'll be a bit pissed, ergo, horny. The idea is to get you into his bed in record time. On the plus side he has a modicum of style and, I'd wager, lots of charm, but beware of sleeping with anyone on a first date, no matter how many oysters they try to force down you.

This man does not drink alcohol, ever. He is macro-biotic in the extreme and polishes his cutlery on his napkin, just in case it's contaminated. He talks endlessly about the environment and wears plastic shoes. He cycles every-where, refusing to drive or take any form of public trans-port, thus doing his bit for 'the cause'. He's 35 years old and still lives with his mother.

Yawn. I live by the adage: everything in moderation, including moderation. Next!

He decides to skip the food part of dinner entirely and opts for getting roaring drunk. He veers between morose and euphoric, but is appealing in a 'save me, I think I'm drowning' kind of way. What you mistook for bonhomie when you first met is actually desperation. Generous to a fault, he has the Dudley Moore character Arthur down to a tee. 'Would you like another fish?'

He's an alcoholic. No, you can't save him, don't even try.

He orders a beer, some wine, an adventurous starter, an indulgent main course and some pudding to share with you. Then perhaps he'll order some more wine, coffee and a couple of brandies. He's funny, charming and seems to really listen to what you have to say. Just as the coffee arrives he reaches across the table for your hand and tells you how beautiful you look tonight.

He's lovely, interested and interesting. He's in no hurry to bolt down dinner in a bid to seduce you tonight, he's here to have a good time. You actually want *this one to make a pass at you! (Yes, this really can happen, great dates do exist, you just gotta keep looking.)*

I asked my date what she wanted to drink.
She said, 'Oh, I guess I'll have champagne.'
I said 'Guess again.'

ANON

Traits to watch out for in a woman on a first date.

(Ladies, do you recognise yourselves?)

After several glasses of champagne, this little madam orders the most expensive dish on the menu before necking as much wine as she can drink and then finishing off with a pudding meant for two. She scoffs the lot, as well as all the after-dinner chocolates. Her only topic of conversation is herself and her pathological desire to acquire, by fair means or foul, anything from Gucci.

A greedy guts with definite gold-digging tendencies. Suggest you go Dutch and then run away.

She requests still, ambient, spring water and a starter of vegetable consommé followed by a main course of mixed salad – hold the croutons and absolutely no dressing. This fresh air feast will be followed by a protracted absence while she goes to the loo. She is very quiet all evening, in fact, she hardly says a word and doesn't seem to be listening to you either. Don't take it personally, it's not you, she's just exhausted!

She's anorexic. Conversely, if when she comes back from the loo she orders two desserts, scoffs the lot and then disappears off to the loo again, she's bulimic.

This little minx acts all girly and helpless and insists you order for her, you big strong man, you. She spends the whole of dinner gazing adoringly into your eyes and agrees with everything you say. Her pièce de résistance? Asking how many kids you'd like and how you feel about living in the country.

She's desperate for a husband and 2.2 children and assuming that this is not forthcoming within the first two weeks of knowing you, has the potential to turn into a bunny boiler. I bet you anything she's already trying on your surname for size . . . run!

Before she even reaches the table she's downed a couple of Margaritas (no salt) amid lots of nervous chatter. She then has a couple of glasses of wine with a light but daring starter, followed by a main course that she seemed to really want but it now appears she's not so keen; she's pushing it around her plate rather than actually eating it.

She's nervous and what's more she really likes you, hence the rather un-cool initial chattering. As the evening progresses and she chills out you will be captivated by her intelligence, amusing conversation and feminine charms. Shame about losing her appetite, especially as once she's home the first thing she will do is make a bacon sandwich.

There's one more rule of thumb: if he covertly flirts with the waitress it's a sure sign he'll be unfaithful. Harsh, but fair. If she flirts with a waiter, she's bored. But hey, don't worry, in my experience that means she'll be picking up the tab.

Assuming the date has gone well and we want to see him again, bringing the evening to a close can be a tricky business. How far should one go on a first date, especially if we really like the guy?

At the end of any date there is always that awkward 'will he kiss me, won't he kiss me?' moment. Suddenly he does and when it's a magical, waves crashing on the shore, full blown Hollywood-style smooch we really don't want to bring the evening to an end as our hearts pound and we get more than a little hot under the collar. The question is, should we hold back or should we abandon ourselves to the moment and follow our more primal instincts and go with the flow? There is, of course, no right or wrong answer, we just have to do what we feel is right for us.

All this talk of should we, shouldn't we, leads me to thinking about one-night stands: why we have them and if they really are all that enjoyable?

ONE-NIGHT STANDS

The Fast Food of the Relationship Banquet

I'm always looking for meaningful one-night stands.

DUDLEY MOORE

Ah, yes, the one-night stand.

I'm sure we all have cherished memories of the dawn walk of shame: teetering along on our 5in spike-heel Manolo's, double-shot latte in hand, wearing last night's crumpled barfly outfit (comprising of teeny top and even teenier skirt), and with mascara streaked halfway down our faces. All in all the image of an unmade bed on stilts desperately trying to be invisible whilst actually sticking out like a sore thumb, attracting knowing looks from those more sensible souls heading for the gym or the office, as one really should be at this time of morning, making us feel rather akin to an alley cat coming home with the milk.

I have never understood what compels us to engage in the somewhat empty activity that is the one-night stand. It must be, by definition, fairly average or surely we would want to repeat it? (There are, of course, exceptions to this rule: those times when it *was* wonderful but circumstances prevailed, although these instances are few and far between.)

Don't get me wrong, I as much as the next girl recognise the pull of that 'eyes across a crowded room' moment where two people are inexplicably drawn to each other and suddenly your knickers are on fire. Raw passion, bring it on.

I know lots of people whose entire sexual raison d'être is built around casual encounters with strangers. They regularly pick up random cute, fun strangers for a one-nighter, fully aware it's not the start of anything; indeed, in most cases, the act of copulation signifies the *end*. Somewhat embarrassingly, should these two bon viveurs accidentally bump into each other sometime further down the line they either ignore each other totally, or mumble a quick hello and head for the nearest exit, despite having been as close as two people can be and having shared bodily fluids.

A one-night stand is rather like eating too much junk food: good at the time, but you feel like crap afterwards.

Leaping into bed with someone too soon can kill off a potential relationship quicker than anything I know. It tends to happen at the dead of night after two people who hardly know each other share one too many cocktails. Having done the deed, one of them has to take the walk of shame as they've ended up on the opposite side of town from where they live and they have to be up for work/an early meeting/their kids, etc. Next morning both parties are a little fuzzy about who they were with and what happened. To quote one particular friend, 'if you can't remember it, it doesn't count.'

Whilst a part of me can see the argument for uncomplicated, no-strings sex I also think if you have a great first date, or even if you've just met someone in a bar and you like them enough to play hide the sausage, why not get to know them a little better first?

I have a couple of girlfriends (names withheld to protect the not-so-innocent) who, frankly, would love to be in a proper relationship. They are attractive, sexy, intelligent women with great jobs and are much sought after by the opposite sex. They are actively looking for something longer term, yet they scupper every possibility of a man asking them out by dragging him home the first time they meet (in some cases quite literally dragging), having a quick bonk and then getting upset when he doesn't call or send flowers the next day. Whaddaya expect? Why buy the cow when you can get the milk for free?

It's my theory that all men are hunters; they enjoy the chase, it satisfies some primeval macho need within them. Equally, just as Mother Nature intended, women love being pursued. So why should we mess up this vitally important component of the courtship ritual?

Men *enjoy* the thrill of the chase. Conversely, women love being pursued and, come on ladies admit it, we all enjoy playing a little hard to get. So what is the point of this 'sniff, sniff, you're nice' instant gratification?

One-night stands may well have their attraction, but when we are actively seeking 'the one' perhaps we should consider taking a little time to woo and be wooed?

I have been on more laps than a napkin.

MAE WEST

For those mornings when we crash through the front door at 6am feeling a little worse for wear due to lack of sleep, far too many cocktails and the ensuing walk of shame, here's a little schedule that I promise will have you on your feet, at the office on time and back to your sparkling old self in the wink of an eye.

1. The very first thing that must be done once you've staggered through the door is to put the kettle on. Secondly, pour yourself a small glass of water, preferably at room temperature, and mix in 4 drops of milk thistle tincture and a good squeeze of lemon. Down it in one. (Funnily enough in much the same way you were downing tequila shots a few hours ago.)

2. Whilst waiting for the kettle to boil remove all clothing, including jewellery, and take a hot shower. Just before you finish, turn off the hot tap completely and blast your senses awake with 20 seconds of icy cold water. It may sound barbaric, but it works.

3. Before drying off, moisturise your entire body with baby oil (nothing makes your skin feel softer and it must be applied whilst you're still wet), and then wrap yourself up in the biggest, fluffiest towel you possess.

4. The kettle will have boiled by now, so brew an exceptionally strong pot of coffee and rustle up two slices of toast topped with honey and mashed banana. Curl up in front of breakfast television until feelings of wellbeing return. (Caffeine, carbohydrates and potassium, found in bananas, are the holy trinity of hangover cures. Watching telly simply diverts your attention away from how crap you feel.)

5. When you feel human enough to get dressed, choose your outfit for the day carefully; make sure it's something you feel good in, preferably tailored and razor-sharp. If at all possible avoid your usual route to work if it involves crowded buses or, worse, the tube; either walk or take a cab, stopping off on the way for a large fresh carrot and green apple juice. A little pampering and indulgence intensifies feelings of wellbeing which will in turn lessen both the hangover and any residual negative feelings resulting from the walk of shame.

Yes, I know, never again.

INFATUATION

❦

Down the slippery slidey slope we go
What will we find there?
God only knows!

Bewitched, Bothered and Bewildered.

LORENZ HART

So, how are the two of you doing?

You've been on two or three dates and, frankly, it's been a long time since you liked anyone this much and every time you think of him you get butterflies and, well, he's just so wonderful.

Congratulations! You're infatuated.

Doesn't it feel amazing? You are seeing glimpses of the possibility, of the chance of something really special and it's hard to stop smiling.

Welcome then to the start of the really good bit of The Beginning. You can forget all about holding back now, it's time to take a leap of faith and go for it in every way. The brakes are off.

The sight of her face . . . together with the maddening
fragrance of food evoked an emotion of wild
tenderness and hunger in him that was unutterable.

THOMAS WOLFE

At this stage food is a major player in the game that is Lust and Seduction, despite the nausea that comes with infatuation and ensures that eating is the last thing on our minds. Our appetites wane, we have the attention span of dyslexic ducks and all we can think about is *'Them'*.

Within the hormonally-charged delirium of this as yet unfulfilled lust, food is a very powerful weapon to wield in order to communicate our desire. Can you think of anything more sensual than preparing and sharing a meal with a person you've got the hots for? Especially food that must be eaten à deux, preferably with fingers – all that licking and sucking is surely the culinary equivalent of pornography.

At The Beginning food is something to be nibbled on, picked at, grazed upon and fed to each other. It is provocative and sensual (thus fuelling the already highly-charged sexual tension between fledgling lovers), an instrument of nourishment not only for our bodies, but also subconsciously for feeding our ardour. The morsels upon which we feast are a suggestion of our passion.

You look puzzled. Let me explain.

There is a theory – admittedly it's *my* theory – that suggests how and what we choose to eat are personal barometers for how we make love. A neat, picky, fastidious eater, strictly meat-and-two-overcooked-veg-with-no-herbs-or-seasoning type is unlikely to make love in quite the same way as a finger-licking gourmand with a weakness for exotic spices, caviar and anything with butter and garlic.

Alongside food, candlelight, little black dresses, giggling, flowers, double-cuffed shirts, high heels, taxis, lashings of mascara, cocktails, cigars, champagne, soft music, perfume, fine wines, holding hands, aftershave and post-dinner liqueurs are all part of new lovers' repast.

THE SEDUCTION DINNERS

Food to Entice, Excite and Enrapture

> *To a man, offering him food is like*
> *offering him a breast.*
>
> ANON

 The first time we invite that someone special to dinner it's not really about dinner, more a preamble to something we are far more excited about, but The Dinner is our casting couch, our siren call, so we need to make sure it's right. The menu should be simple and sensuous, light, but luxurious enough to be a little naughty and seductive.

Make sure the table looks good, nothing too formal; romantic, flirty and sexy is what we are looking for. Use flowers and candles in abundance. Lots of tea lights scattered around the room can be extremely effective. (Honey, everyone looks good by candlelight.) The use of pretty crockery, yards of cutlery, champagne, wine and water glasses, rose petals scattered on the tablecloth, finger bowls for sticky fingers, unusual breads with a dish of balsamic and olive oil for dipping and crisp white napkins all combine to create a feeling of luxury and pampering. Get dressed up; wear your sexiest dress and skyscraper heels. Perfect takes a tad longer, but it is worth the effort.

Serve the best champagne you can afford. Nothing, and I mean nothing, sets the tone for a romantic evening like a glass of fizz. Don't be tempted to tamper with it, champagne cocktails are wonderful but lethal and you will both get too drunk, too fast. Hey, we have an agenda here!

The purpose of the Seduction Dinner is to create the basis of an evening that will impress the hell out of your chosen one whilst being relatively easy to shop for and that can be prepared in advance. This is crucial as it allows you all the time in the world to get yourself sexy . . . take a long bath with a glass of champagne and pamper yourself. You're worth it.

> *I will not eat oysters; I want my food dead,*
> *Not sick, not wounded . . . dead.*

WOODY ALLEN

Whilst I adore the indomitable Woody Allen, he is really missing the point here. Oysters are the ultimate aphrodisiac, the science bit of which revolves around the high levels of zinc they are said to contain. To be frank, the science bit bores me, all I know is that these little beauties are capable of conjuring up a feeling of luxury and seduction like no other food in the world. Plump, moist and tasting exactly like the sea, they sit nestled in their pretty little iridescent, mother-of-pearl shells, just waiting to be sucked and slurped – the very act of which is so highly erotically charged it is akin to foreplay. They are simply a *must* at any Seduction Dinner, and I know of nothing else that marries so well with ice-cold champagne.

Get yourself down to a good fishmonger and buy a dozen of the freshest and finest oysters they have. Buy them already shucked and on the half shell (any good fish-monger will be happy to do this for you) and run straight home, popping them in the fridge as soon as you get there. Serve these wondrous morsels on crushed ice, with a splash of Tabasco, as a preamble to dinner . . . Oysters and champagne scream *seduction*! In fact, as I write this I can't help but feel a little envious, can I come to dinner too?

For the squeamish amongst you, and for those of you who, alas, agree with Mr Allen and simply cannot eat oysters, substitute with smoked salmon served on triangles of buttered brown bread, a squeeze of lemon and a sprinkling of paprika. For those non-fishy people, buy a small amount of good foie gras pâté and spread on thinly-sliced, lightly-toasted baguette and top with thin slivers of cornichons (baby gherkins to you and me).

Whatever you choose to serve as an amuse-bouche it should be a small, luxurious, taste explosion to complement the champagne and kick the evening off with a rather illustrious bang!

Seduction Menu 1

A Salad of Parma Ham with Figs, Mascarpone and Rocket

Linguini with Lobster and Champagne

Iced Raspberries with Hot White Chocolate Sauce

The Salad:

2 ripe figs; 4 slices Parma ham; 2 tbsp mascarpone cheese; a grating of fresh nutmeg; 2 large handfuls of rocket; sea salt and freshly ground black pepper. Balsamic vinegar and olive oil to dress.

An effortless and unbelievably gorgeous starter. Take 2 figs and cut a cross into them about three-quarters of the way down. Squeeze their bottoms gently to open them up and expose the inside. Wrap a slice of Parma ham around each fig, fill the inside with a spoon of mascarpone and top with a grating of nutmeg. Bake in a medium oven, 180°C (350°F) until the mascarpone is bubbling, about 5 minutes; serve on a bed of rocket which has been drizzled with balsamic vinegar and olive oil. Give the whole thing a good grind of black pepper and sea salt then tear up the remaining slices of ham into ribbons and scatter onto each plate. Serve with warm crusty bread.

The Linguini:

To serve someone lobster is to spoil them utterly. If they were in any doubt of your intentions, this dish should spell it out for them.

> A 1kg (2½lb) lobster; 2 cloves garlic, finely chopped; a small fresh red chilli, deseeded and finely sliced; 3 knobs unsalted butter; 2 tbsp olive oil; 400g (14oz) tin of plum tomatoes; a large glass of champagne; a small glass of water; 250g (9oz) linguini, cooked al dente; 1 handful flat leaf parsley, finely chopped; sea salt and freshly ground pepper.

If you have bought your lobster live, plunge it into boiling water for 15 minutes then remove. (If you have bought a cooked, ready-to-go lobster, you're a wuss!) When cooled, crack and remove all the meat from the shell, making sure there are no splinters.

To make the sauce, fry the shells and legs in the olive oil and 2 knobs of butter over a medium heat with the garlic and chilli. Add the tomatoes, a large glass of champagne and a small glass of water, gently boil on a high heat to reduce the alcohol (for about 3 minutes), then simmer gently for 1 hour. Allow to cool. Pass the sauce through a fine sieve twice, checking for splinters. Place in a clean pan, add a final knob of butter and season to taste. Add the cooked pasta to the sauce and toss it until well covered. Add the lobster at the moment of serving, toss lightly keeping the lobster meat visible on top of the pasta and serve in warmed bowls with a sprinkling of parsley.

The Berries:

This really could not be easier, but it tastes like it took a great deal of effort. Prepare the sauce in advance so that all you have to do before serving is place the raspberries in individual glasses and reheat the sauce. Serve the Framboise frozen in shot glasses, it finishes off the dish to perfection and gives it quite a kick!

A pack of frozen raspberries (or fresh ones, frozen), about 150g (5oz) per person; 600g (1½lb) of good-quality white chocolate; 600ml (1 pint) double cream; 2 shots of Framboise (raspberry liqueur, optional).

Break up the chocolate and place with the cream in a bowl placed over a pan of simmering water for 20–30 minutes, stirring every so often until the chocolate has melted and the sauce is hot. (If prepared in advance, reheat the sauce in the same way). Five minutes before serving, place the berries in your prettiest dessert glasses or on dessert plates and leave at room temperature for 5 minutes. Cover the berries generously with the sauce and serve immediately with the shots of Framboise on the side.

Seduction Menu 2

Prawns with Garlic, Butter and Lemon

Roasted Swordfish on a Tomato, Pepper and Red Onion Salsa

Dark Chocolate Desire

The Prawns:

8–10 raw tiger prawns per person, depending on the size of the prawns (and your wallet); 2 tbsp butter; 1 tbsp olive oil; 2 cloves of finely chopped garlic; the juice of a lemon; a further large knob of butter; a handful of finely chopped parsley; sea salt and freshly ground pepper.

When cooking the prawns do so with the heads on or, if you wish, remove the heads and butterfly them by cutting through the back of the shell to remove the black vein and opening them flat. Do not remove all of the shell as it adds to the flavour of the sauce and anyway, what could be sexier than peeling a prawn for your lover?

Gently warm the butter, oil and the garlic in a frying pan large enough to hold all the prawns and nice enough to be put on the table. When the butter is foaming, toss the prawns in, turning them as they go pink and cook for about 3 minutes (slightly less if butterflied), then add the lemon juice and the rest of the butter. Allow the sauce to come back to a sizzle, adjust the seasoning and sprinkle with chopped parsley.

The prawns in all their hot, sticky gorgeousness should be whisked off the hob to the table whilst still spitting and sizzling and should be served in the very pan in which they were cooked. Eat them with your fingers and serve with some crusty bread to mop up those garlicky buttery juices.

The Swordfish:
A light and healthy dish with big flavours to excite the most jaded of palates.

2 swordfish steaks about 200g (7oz) each, about 1cm thick; olive oil.

The Salsa:
6 really ripe plum tomatoes, deseeded and finely chopped; 1 red pepper, deseeded and finely chopped; 2 medium red chillies, finely sliced; 1 tbsp of capers, chopped; a small red

onion, finely chopped; a clove of garlic, finely chopped; a
handful of parsley, finely chopped; a handful of fresh basil
leaves, finely chopped; 2 anchovy fillets, chopped; 6 tbsp of
good olive oil; 3 tbsp of lemon juice combined with 2 tbsp of
runny honey; sea salt and freshly ground black pepper.

Combine all the salsa ingredients in a bowl, season with
salt and pepper, cover with a cloth and leave for at least
2 hours at room temperature for the flavours to infuse.

Preheat a grill pan or heavy-bottomed frying pan until very
hot, rub each of the swordfish steaks with olive oil, season
with salt and pepper on both sides and place in the pan. Cook
on a very high heat for two to three minutes on each side so
the fish is a little charred, take care not to burn it.

To serve, place a couple of large spoonfuls of salsa on a
plate and top with the swordfish. Serve with a mixed green
salad dressed with the juices of the pan, a little olive oil
and a squeeze of lemon juice and some good crusty bread.

Dark Chocolate Desire:

Time for something sweet. A bitter chocolate dessert –
rich, silky and positively illicit. A little of this goes a long
way, so serve in tiny espresso cups.

285ml (10oz) single cream; 200g (7oz) bitter dark chocolate
(70 per cent cocoa solids); 2 egg yolks, beaten; 3 tbsp
brandy; 20g (1oz) butter, 2 Amaretto biscotti.

Heat the cream in a saucepan until nearly boiling. Set aside for a minute or two. Break up the chocolate into small pieces and combine with the cream, stir until melted. Beat in the egg yolks and brandy and stir until mixture is creamy. Allow to cool a little then add the butter and mix until smooth. Pour into the espresso cups and place in the fridge to set. (Should the mixture separate when you add the butter, allow the mixture to cool a little more then whisk in a little cold milk until you have a smooth consistency.) Just before serving, grind the Amaretti biscuits into a dust and sprinkle over the top of the cups, allowing the residue to fall on the saucers.

Seduction Menu 3

Frisée with a Warm Pancetta, Balsamic and Honey Dressing

Chargrilled Rump Steak with Béarnaise Sauce and Pommes Frites

Caffé Affogato

I have known grown men to swoon over this particular menu. It sounds easy, but done well nothing can touch it. As a woman cooking for man I can highly recommend the results you will achieve by putting on your pinny and serving him some good, old-fashioned red meat. To keep the menu balanced the starter and dessert are very light: after all, we need him to stay awake. A good South Australian Shiraz goes really well with this.

The Salad:

2 large handfuls crisp frisée lettuce; 8 slices pancetta or 6 slices dry-cured, smoked streaky bacon; 6 small shallots, peeled and quartered; 3 tbsp pine nuts; 6 tbsp olive oil; 3 tbsp balsamic vinegar mixed with 2 tbsp runny honey; sea salt and freshly ground black pepper.

Fry the pancetta or bacon in a hot frying pan until crisp, remove and set aside. Add the olive oil, shallots and pine nuts to the pan and cook until the onions are soft and sweet (about 10 minutes over a lowish flame), keep the contents of the pan moving. Return the bacon or pancetta to the pan and toss everything around, turn off the heat. Place the frisee in a big salad bowl and add the contents of the pan and the balsamic-honey mixture. Season with salt and pepper and toss the salad until all the components are distributed evenly and serve immediately with some warm crusty bread or garlic bread to mop up the dressing.

The Béarnaise Sauce:

1 small shallot, peeled and finely chopped; 3 tbsp white wine or tarragon vinegar; 6 black whole peppercorns; 3 sprigs of

tarragon, roughly chopped including stalks; 2 egg yolks whisked with 1 tsp Dijon mustard; 150g (5oz) softened butter cut into ½in cubes.

Put the chopped shallot into a small saucepan with the vinegar, peppercorns and tarragon. Bring to the boil and reduce it to a tablespoon or so of liquor (don't move from the stove as this does not take very long), pass this liquor through a sieve or tea strainer to get rid of the bits and bobs and put to one side. Put the egg yolks and the mustard into a glass bowl and place over a saucepan of gently simmering water, the bowl should fit snugly on the top of the pan. Whisk the vinegar reduction into the egg yolks, keeping the water under them simmering, then slowly start to add the cubes of butter one at a time, whisking constantly until the sauce is thick and velvety. Turn off the heat halfway through adding the butter, as the sauce must not get too hot. (Should disaster strike and the sauce separates, remove the bowl from the heat, add a spoonful of boiling water from the pan and whisk it like a mad thing. It should right itself.) Once the heat is off, add a little salt if necessary. To keep warm, leave it in the bowl over the pan of water (no flame) covered with a cloth and whisk occasionally.

The Pommes Frites:
Ok, here's the bit where you cheat. I buy my pomme frites very thin and frozen because I hate, detest and abhor the

smell of deep-fat frying, I think it's the least romantic smell in the whole wide world *ever*. So, I oven-cook them on an oiled baking tray with a severe grinding of sea salt in a fairly hot oven. He will never ever know, especially if you undo a button on your oh-so-sexy top whilst serving them.

What can I tell you? The female of the species is by far deadlier and more cunning than the male.

The Steak:

2 rump steaks about an inch thick and 300g (11oz) in weight; olive oil; a garlic clove; sea salt and freshly ground pepper.

(Please get your steaks from a reputable old-fashioned butcher's shop where the meat is cut from the rump in front of you, not pre-cut and packed in Styrofoam and cling film from a supermarket. Butcher's meat is far superior, it really is worth the effort and the more we support our local shopkeepers, the better chance they have of survival and of not being squeezed out by the superstores. Lecture over, enough said.)

Preheat your ridged, cast-iron grill pan or, failing that, a heavy-bottomed frying pan until very hot, having first rubbed it with the garlic clove. Coat either side of your steaks with olive oil and a grinding of black pepper (some people prefer to salt their steak at the end of the cooking process believing it preserves the juices of the meat, I'm not sure it makes that much difference, but it's up to you). Place the steaks on the grill pan and press down hard. Let them cook for 2 minutes without moving them, this will ensure you achieve that lovely chargrilled, slightly crunchy exterior. Turn over after the 2 minutes are up, preferably using tongs (if you stab your meat with a fork you will sacrifice your juices), once again press down and cook for a further 2 minutes. This will give you a medium-rare steak, though it's impossible to pinpoint the exact timing due to thickness of the cut and the hanging time of the meat, etc, the only real way to know is to cut into it a little towards the middle of steak. If you like your steak a little more well done, keep it in the pan, turning it every minute or so. Once cooked, turn off the heat and allow the steaks to rest for a couple of minutes. Serve with the pommes frites and Béarnaise sauce and some watercress dressed with the pan juices. Sit back, enjoy and watch him drool.

Caffé Affogato

Translated literally, this means 'drowned coffee' and really could not be easier to make. Make some strong filter or espresso coffee, if you're lucky enough to own an espresso-making machine pour enough for 2 small cups into a jug and add 2 tsps of sugar. Place a generous dollop of ice-cream into each of 2 dessert glasses, pour over some of your favourite liqueur or, failing that, whatever you have handy – brandy, Amaretto, Cointreau all make fine additions. Top with the coffee and serve with some fancy little biscuits bought especially for the occasion.

Quite apart from being delicious, this clever little pudding gets the whole dessert, coffee and brandy thing out of the way in one hit.

APHRODISIACS

The Food of Love

The food of love
He eats nothing but does love
and that breeds hot blood
and hot blood begets hot thoughts
and hot thoughts beget hot deeds
and hot deeds is love.

WILLIAM SHAKESPEARE

 An aphrodisiac is anything at all that piques our sexual interest. Everyone has their own personal catalogue of food that inexplicably turns them on. It really is a case of one horny man's meat being another man's total turnoff.

It's all about personal experience and memory. For

example, if you had your first sexual encounter having just had baked beans on toast for dinner then that humble repast will be forever imprinted in your memory as a sexual trigger, which is exactly what an aphrodisiac is all about.

The mind boggles!

There are also those generic aphrodisiacs that seem to work for everyone, goodness knows why. For example, we have already ascertained that in the case of oysters they are loaded with zinc, which is known to increase energy and assist fertility, but is it really that scientific or could it be purely psychological, caused by our wicked imaginations playing tricks on us?

I have put together a collection of some pretty powerful aphrodisiacs for your delight and delectation. Experiment, and see what works for you.

N.B. The best aphrodisiac of all is love. Passion, where love is also present, knows no bounds and has no limits.

Divine Aphrodite, much celebrated lover of laughter,
companion of Bacchus, whose bliss is abundant,
patroness of feasts which last for nights.

HOMER, THE ILIAD

Now, here is an interesting thing. A recent sex study in America involving a group of men tested penile blood flow in response to various aromas. Apparently, the more erotic they found the smell, the greater the reaction. With me so far? The stuff they tested included, amongst other things, expensive perfumes, female pheromones, suntan lotion, various flowers and freshly ground coffee. They found out that the biggest turn on, the one that set the blood rushing, was none other than the spice cinnamon (now known as Love Dust), which by pure coincidence (or is it?) was the signature spice of the greatest female seductress of all time, Aphrodite, goddess of love.

Apparently, when she needed a little assistance with her seduction technique (despite her well-documented and considerable charms), she simply sprinkled a little cinnamon dust onto her victim's dinner and the poor man was toast. Putty in her hands. It has to be worth a try!

Here are a few more:

It is mooted that caviar works very well, it's the zinc thing again, though I personally believe it's because it is so damn expensive you feel spoilt and special, ergo, horny, just being around the stuff. Also, any kind of shellfish: prawns, lobster, mussels, scallops – all that prising, peeling, licking and sucking does it for me every time.

With regards fruit, I love grapes because you get to drape a bunch of them over your mouth and devour them in the manner of a Roman orgy; strawberries, because they fit so nicely into a champagne glass and are the perfect fruit to dip in melted chocolate and feed to your lover; figs, because, well, I won't go into detail, suffice to say they bear a startling resemblance to female genitalia when cut in half; but the high priestess of aphrodisiac fruits, as quoted in the *Kama Sutra*, is the pomegranate. It was also the sacred fruit of Aphrodite, and we know what a little minx she was! For my money, if sex were a fruit it would be a mango: the taste, texture and perfume drive this woman to distraction.

Asparagus is also extremely effective. Again, I think it's the licking and sucking quota that makes it so sexy, rather than the actual taste. Of course, we cannot forget the truffle, the smell of which drives men and women wild; that musky aroma is capable of arousing even the most reticent lover.

N.B. If you are seeking a guaranteed successful seduction I will avail you of my secret weapon, a menu so packed with aphrodisiacs it should carry a health warning.

Culinary Viagra

Start with some stems of lightly steamed asparagus served with hollandaise for dipping, follow this with a steaming bowl of tagliatelle dressed with nothing but a large knob of butter, a dusting of Parmesan and finished off with shavings of fresh white truffle. Dessert is slices of mango and pomegranate seeds sprinkled with cinnamon. You should, of course, serve nothing but champagne through-out the whole meal.

Use this menu wisely and sparingly, as it will provoke nothing short of a sexual frenzy.

Herbs and spices are jammed with aphrodisiacal powers. Cinnamon, as we have discussed, is top of the list, also ginger for male fertility and nutmeg for staying power. Ginseng can apparently fuel our sexuality in the manner of rabid rabbits, and saffron, here's one for the girls, assists in arousal as it ensures our erogenous zones are ultra sensitive.

I find one of the most effective, sure-fire aphrodisiacs is champagne. It gets you squiffy quite fast and one tends to lose all one's inhibitions, along with one's knickers. Clearly all alcohol can be used to the same effect, but a pint of bitter does not quite have the same ring to it nor, I imagine, the same results.

My family has an old recipe that is reserved expressly for honeymooners. As newlyweds my parents spent a few days of their honeymoon on my grandfather's farm near Parma. While they were there my great-grand-mother, Nonna Marianna – in a bid to assist the baby-making process – would knock up her version of an aphrodisiac every morning and deliver it to the happy couple at breakfast time, placing it outside their door with a sharp rap of her knuckles to alert them to its presence.

The recipe was passed down to her from her great-grandmother and a few years ago when my sister and brother-in-law were passing a few days of *their* honeymoon at the farm before their grand tour of Italy, it was my mother who was at hand to prepare for them this very special family tradition.

Nonna Marianna had 12 kids and swore that each one was due to this recipe.

Uova Sbattute Luna di Miele (Honeymoon Eggs)

4 egg yolks; 4 tbsp caster sugar; 4 tbsp Marsala.

Whisk the egg yolks and sugar together until you have a pale gold, creamy froth then add the Marsala and a huge pinch of love.

It's kind of like an uncooked Zabaglione, although much lighter and without the Savoyard biscuits.

The happy couple are meant to share a bowl of this every morning to ensure virility in him and fertility in her.

N.B. My Nonna died at the ripe old age of 97, and a wiser woman I have yet to meet.

PINK CLOUD

ॐ

Rose-Tinted Rapture

Knowing you is such delicious torment.
RALPH WALDO EMERSON

My, oh my, things are going well. You have now crossed the relationship Rubicon and are officially in that delicious stage commonly referred to as 'Pink Cloud'.

You lucky people.

You have so much to look forward to. This is my favourite bit (which explains a lot about me). By now it's clear that you are both very keen, although neither of you has actually said anything you can just feel it and see it written in each other's eyes.

You are slowly starting to discover each other's characteristics and foibles, layer by layer, much like peeling an onion, and you get a real kick out of doing fairly mundane things together like, supermarket shopping, travelling to work, going to the gym, etc. They are all so much more fun, a deux.

Operating in Pink Cloud ensures that when you go out to dinner it seems for all the world as if the two of you are the only people in the restaurant, existing in your own little bubble. Invariably you are the last to leave and the waiters usually end up sweeping up around you, but even then you are having so much fun you can't bear the evening to end and search out a late night bar so you can carry on talking and touching, thrilled by the simple fact of being together.

You have gone from only seeing each other on Saturday nights to spending the whole of Sunday together in blessed and blissful Pink Cloud rapture. For the culinary goddess this presents the perfect opportunity to dazzle him, but it *does* mean getting just a little organised in preparation for those dreamy weekends you now spend joined at the hip.

EASY LIKE SUNDAY MORNING

❦

Brilliant Brunches

*Here's to me and here's to you and here's
to love and laughter.
I'll be true as long as you and not one moment after.*

Irish Breakfast Toast

Your eyes flutter open, it's Sunday morning –
well, just, it's 11.55am. You snuggle closer to your
still sleeping bed mate, sigh contentedly and let your mind
wander.

It has been an incredible few weeks. Suddenly, life is a
roller coaster – delightful, bewitching and perhaps just a
little insane. It's early days but you think this one could be
the one.

Last night was wonderful; you went to a couple of bars,

had supper in a wonderful French restaurant where you held hands and gazed into each other's eyes, barely touching your food. Later, he took you dancing and when you eventually got home you opened a bottle of wine, listened to music, talked until dawn then climbed into bed and made love. It was unequivocally the most magical and perfect date you have ever had.

A blissful, lazy Sunday stretches before you. The papers have been delivered (three sagacious broadsheets plus your must-have tabloid gossip rag without which Sunday would not be complete) and then he stirs. A kiss, more cuddles, he speaks . . . 'I'm starving.'

And because you are such a clever bunny and planned ahead, you have the makings of the perfect Sunday brunch. How impressive?

You're gonna blow his socks off!

The Perfect Sunday Brunch for Two

Ok, so you just woke up and frankly don't feel too much like having a marathon session in the kitchen. No problem, the idea is that brunch is something that is easily thrown together and satisfies that Sunday afternoon 'sort-of hangover' feeling, combined with the fact that you were too starry-eyed to eat your dinner last night and you're running on empty.

First things first. Before you even attempt to get up and do anything you need coffee, and lots of it. Bicker about who's going to get up and make it and drink the first cup in bed. There, there, you should be feeling better already.

Take a shower, get dressed and wander into the kitchen. Still feeling a bit blurry? I know exactly what you both need. The best Sunday morning pick-me-up known to man. I have no idea how it works, I just know it does.

Bloody Mary

4 shots vodka; ½ litre (¾ pint) chilled tomato juice; celery salt; 4 dashes each Worcestershire sauce, Tabasco; juice of half a lemon; 1 tsp horseradish; ice cubes; two 6in sticks of celery; freshly ground black pepper.

Combine everything but the pepper, ice and the celery in a jug and give it a good mix. Place the ice cubes and the celery in two highball glasses, pour in the Bloody Mary, top with a grind of pepper and enjoy.

Bet that hits the spot. Sip it whilst preparing brunch and by the time it's ready, you'll be ready, too.

Right then, it's now probably around 2ish, definitely time to start cooking.

Lay the table as you would for dinner: mats, champagne flutes, napkins, glasses, cups, side plates with butter knives, maybe even some fresh flowers. If it *looks* special it will *feel* special. Have a breadbasket lined with a napkin ready for the toast and muffins so when they are ready you can cover them to keep warm. Try some mellow music whilst you're cooking; Ella Fitzgerald, Nina Simone, Joss Stone or the king of mellow himself, Marvin Gaye, would be just perfect.

Sunday Brunch Menu 1

Prosecco with Fresh Orange or Peach Juice

Scrambled Eggs, Smoked Salmon, Wholegrain Toast

Toasted English Muffins, Jam or Honey

Fresh Mangos

Prosecco is a dry, Italian sparkling wine, although any good-quality chilled sparkler will do. To make the peach juice, liquidise the flesh of 4 peaches in a blender.

The Scrambled Eggs:

5 eggs lightly beaten; 1 tbsp butter; salt and pepper; 2 slices buttered wholegrain toast.

First prepare everything except for the toast, which should be done at the same time as the eggs. Lay the smoked salmon on one side of the plate and sprinkle with paprika and a little lemon. Heat the butter in a saucepan and when foaming add the eggs. Using a wooden spoon, stir like mad until the eggs are cooked but still soft and creamy then turn off the heat and stir in another knob of butter. Serve on the toast with the salmon.

Sunday Brunch Menu 2

Once again, start with sparkling wine and your choice of juice – there is something wonderfully decadent about drinking fizz with brunch. I reckon a little Frank Sinatra would go down a storm with this, or perhaps a bit of R. Kelly or any other soulful R&B brotha wouldn't go amiss.

But what could be better on a Sunday morning than a properly-made bacon sandwich? The smell of cooking bacon is enough to get anyone out of bed and into the kitchen. This is no ordinary sandwich, it's Sandwich Heaven.

The Bacon Sandwich:

10 slices of top-quality, dry-cured bacon (from a good butcher rather than packaged bacon from a supermarket); sliced mature cheddar; 1 ripe beef tomato, thinly sliced; 2 tbsp good mayonnaise; 2 tbsp ketchup; lettuce leaves; 2 small ciabatta loaves.

Warm a griddle pan until very hot and cook the bacon for one minute each side – it should be a little charred. Remove from the pan and keep warm. Cut the ciabatta loaves in half, place cut-side down onto the griddle pan and toast on either side until golden. Spread some mayo on the bottom half of the loaf, lay some cheese on the top, then the bacon then the tomato and finally some lettuce. Squeeze the whole thing together and leave whole. That's what I call a bacon sandwich!

Sunday Brunch Menu 3

Drum roll, please. I didn't particularly want to include this dish because, even though I love it, it can be a little fiddly, but I really had no choice as so many people, when asked, said it would be their number one choice for a Sunday brunch *if someone else was cooking*!

It is not at all hard to make if you cheat and buy good-quality ready-made hollandaise and if you make your own just make sure you're awake when you do it. You will be adored and venerated if you serve this to an Eggs Benedict Addict; there are lots of them around. Play some soothing classical music whilst preparing this, it's that kind of food.

A Bottle of Champagne
(If you are going to all this trouble, you deserve it)

Eggs Benedict
(I urge you to have at least two each)

Nothing at all
(Perfection is so hard to follow)

Ok, you have a choice, you can cheat and buy the hollandaise ready-made and I have to tell you, I've done it. No one will hold it against you (especially if you hide the packaging and lie!), or you can make it yourself whilst lover boy watches you, marvelling at your culinary genius and pondering on how lucky he was to have found you. Trust me, if he's an addict that is exactly what he will be thinking.

The Eggs:

4 large eggs; 4 slices of bread cut from a large, white loaf about 1in thick; 4 thin slices of good-quality, lean ham.

The Hollandaise:

175g (6oz) of butter; 1 tbsp wine vinegar; 2 tbsp lemon juice; 3 large egg yolks; a pinch of salt.

Melt the butter slowly in a saucepan. Place the wine vinegar and lemon juice in another saucepan and bring to the boil. Blend the egg yolks and salt in a liquidiser then, with the motor running, gradually add the hot lemon juice and vinegar. Do this very slowly to avoid separation, then gradually add the melted butter equally slowly, with the motor running all the time, until the sauce has thickened. To keep it warm, place the finished sauce in a bowl over a pan of boiling water until ready to serve, or if you're cheating now is a good time to throw away the packaging and put your bought hollandaise into a saucepan and gently warm it, adding a tablespoon of butter.

If you have an egg-poaching pan, good for you; I swear by mine and really wouldn't poach an egg without it. If you've bought one especially for this dish, here's the how. Half fill the lower container of the pan with water, place a small knob of butter in each cup and then heat over a medium flame. When the water boils break an egg into each cup and cover the pan. Simmer gently until the eggs are set then turn off the heat, loosen the eggs and they're ready to go. If you're keeping them warm, dot each one with a tiny knob of butter and re-cover.

I'll also give you the old-fashioned method, just in case you don't have an egg poacher. Start off with a good slurp of champagne then half fill a deep frying pan with water and add a pinch of salt and the liquid equivalent of a pinch of vinegar. Go easy on the vinegar or it'll be the only thing you will be able to taste. Bring the water to a gentle boil and swirl it around with a spoon, slipping two eggs at a time into the water whilst it's still moving. Cook gently until lightly set and lift out with a slotted spoon.

Toast the bread and from the centre of each slice cut out a circle slightly bigger than the egg. Put two slices on two warmed plates, don't butter it. On each of the slices of toast place a poached egg topped with a slice of ham, keeping it as neat as you can. Pour hollandaise over the egg and the ham, give it a quick grind of salt and pepper, scatter a little parsley over the whole thing and eat immediately. Eggs Benedict wait for no man.

ROOM SERVICE

℘

A Selection of Post-Coital Suppers

*All the things I really like to do are either illegal,
immoral or fattening.*

ALEXANDER WOOLLCOTT

You were supposed to go out to supper last night
but when he arrived to pick you up you weren't quite
ready, so you both had a pre-dinner cocktail whilst he waited.
Then you had another, and somehow you were finally ready
and, if you say so yourself, you looked damn hot, in fact so
hot that he couldn't keep his hands off you . . . and then *afterwards*, well you had to start all over again.

So you ended up staying home and getting jiggy all night
and now it's 4am and you're both in a relaxed, hazy, loved-
up frame of mind. There's only one thing missing, food. You

fancy something fairly light and easy to prepare, something that you can eat in bed whilst watching re-runs of *Jerry Springer*. Bliss.

Whilst writing *Eat Me* I travelled a lot (the gypsy in my soul ensures I don't stay in one place for too long). I visited Australia, Singapore, Hong Kong, Zurich, Spain, Las Vegas, Thailand, Bali and Italy. I spoke to a lot of people about the book and the subject matter and conducted my own private study about what most people would consider their fantasy meal to be at 4am after a marathon session between the sheets.

Below you will find the results of that study. It was my intention to name each person individually but there were too many of them and it would have been a book in itself. You know who you are, thank you.

P.S. If you are reading this and you are one of those people, *I did it! I got published*!

Suggestions for Post-Coital Suppers from
People all over the World

How to use this list:

Many of the suppers suggested don't require recipes and the ones that do I will outline for you. Of course, the majority of these require very little preparation, thus minimising the amount of time you are away from your lover's arms and leaving you free to argue over the remote control!

What to drink? Whatever you fancy. Anything from a cup of tea or hot chocolate to an ice-cold beer or a glass of champagne, or perhaps just some iced water or a diet coke. It's 4am, have whatever you damn well please!

Eggs:

Lots of you went for eggs, cooked in a hundred different ways: fried and in sandwiches or on toast, scrambled on muffins, or boiled accompanied by hot buttered soldiers or steamed asparagus for dipping. Or you can cook them Italian style: rip a hole in the doughy part of a thick slice of good white bread and fry it in a little olive oil and garlic, breaking the egg into the middle of it. (I've tried it and it's gorgeous.)

Omelettes featured quite prominently too; filled with everything from cheese, bacon, baked beans, mushrooms or fresh herbs to lobster, caviar, banana, apples or, the weirdest one of all, tinned spaghetti. Well, they do say it takes all kinds.

There were also loads of suggestions for poached eggs, baked eggs, raw egg yolks beaten with lots of sugar and Marsala, curried eggs and scotch eggs. Some wanted hard-boiled egg and tomato sandwiches with salad cream, *not* mayonnaise, although there was a suggestion of egg mayonnaise and anchovy sandwiches with cucumber . . .

In conclusion, it would seem that many, many eggs are eaten at 4am.

Pasta:

You want it and you want it *bad*! Actually, thinking about it, it is the perfect 'bed food': no crumbs and requiring only a fork to eat it.

The types of pasta suggested were pretty standard: spaghetti, linguini, farfalle, penne, capellini, tagliatelle and gnocchi. On and on it goes. I suggest you have whatever floats your boat.

Now for the sauces. Some people wanted nothing more than a little garlic and chilli sautéed gently in olive oil a with handful of Parmesan, others wanted a quick tomato sauce; finely chop one onion and one clove of garlic, fry in a little olive oil, add a tin of chopped tomatoes and some dried oregano or fresh basil if you have it, cook over a medium heat for 10 minutes whilst the pasta cooks and finish with some Parmesan and a decent bottle of red. Add a few capers, some chopped black olives and a couple of anchovies and you have a Puttanesca, which literally translated means 'whore's pasta', suggested by quite a few of you. Some wanted their pasta dressed with cream gently warmed with a garlic clove, some cheese and some black pepper, others just wanted a lot of butter and Parmesan. You also suggested ready-made pesto and store-bought sauces for convenience.

Carbonara was popular: combine 100ml (3½fl oz) of cream with 2 egg yolks, some chopped cooked bacon, a good handful of Parmesan and toss it all into just-cooked pasta – the heat of which cooks the egg. There were suggestions for penne with a quick tomato sauce (as above) but with lots of chilli to make an Arrabiata, others just wanted Minestrina (chicken noodle soup); dissolve a couple of chicken stock cubes (choose Monosodium Glutamate-free ones, and avoid that most vicious of white powders that I, and so many others, are allergic to) in some boiling water, pop in some fine egg pasta and simmer gently until the pasta is tender. Add a sprinkling of Parmesan and you have a cuddle in a bowl.

I could literally go on and on, but I think you get the message. Just like in the movie *The Lady and the Tramp*; lovers love pasta.

Frankly, sandwiches, salads and dippy things are my kind of 4am food. I do love a good sandwich and so, it would appear, do you. Fresh bread is imperative – if in doubt either toast it or, if it's a loaf or baguette that is a day or two old, splash it with a little water, stick it in a medium oven for about 5 minutes and then wrap it in a tea towel for a couple more. It works every time.

Sandwiches:

Fillings varied enormously but toasted ham and cheese, bacon, sausage and the ubiquitous chip butty were all major players. Also gammon, ham, hotdogs, all sorts of cheeses, turkey breasts, hamburgers, roast and smoked chicken, Parma ham, steak and onions, smoked salmon, tuna and, of course, eggs were all popular choices.

The more imaginative amongst you wanted salad leaves, ripe sweet tomatoes, cucumber, coleslaw and fresh herbs with their choice of fillings. The diet sandwich of choice these days seems to be tomato with salt and freshly ground pepper, whereas some went to the other extreme and piled their sandwiches sky high with pastrami, bacon and cheese with lettuce, tomato and coleslaw on rye bread, or turkey, bacon, boiled egg, tomato, coleslaw and cucumber on a warm ciabatta (my personal favourite). There were suggestions of pickles, chutneys, mayonnaises, salsas and brown sauces and of peanut butter with banana and honey on brown bread, and fish fingers in crusty rolls with ketchup.

You can put pretty much anything between two slices of bread, and although I drew the line at a couple of suggestions I received I will share them with you anyway. One was fried liver, onions, cheddar cheese and peanut butter on a bagel, another was even worse – dripping (the white glutinous fat that is rendered from roasted meat), with Branston pickle.

Don't even go there.

Salads:

Surprisingly, quite a few of you wanted salads. It was pretty standard stuff: Caesar, Waldorf, Greek and pasta salad (my pet hate) were popular as well as tomato and mozzarella, rocket and Parmesan and, of course, the humble potato salad.

In my opinion the best suggestion came from a French guy living in Australia: stud the inside of two large and meaty portobello mushrooms with garlic, butter and parsley (be generous), then bake at 200°C (400°F) for 20 minutes and serve on half a toasted bap on a bed of rocket, dressed with olive oil and balsamic. Sublime! The other one I loved was a warm salad of ripe plum tomatoes cut in half and cooked in a frying pan over a medium heat with olive oil, crushed garlic, honey and balsamic vinegar until the tomatoes are tender but not sloppy. Serve with lots of crusty bread.

Dippy Things:

Dips were popular; pitta bread with taramasalata, hummus and tsatsiki, big fat oven chips with ketchup and mayonnaise, crisps with ready-made, bought dips, grissini with tapenade, crostini (small slices of toasted baguette topped with diced tomato, olive oil, garlic and basil with salt and pepper), Dolcelatte warmed with a little white wine or mushrooms sautéed in garlic and butter. Tortilla chips covered in melted cheddar (use the microwave), sour cream, sliced jalapeños and guacamole was a big hit, as well as grilled sausages dipped in ketchup and pâté with crusty bread.

Fast Things:

Heinz tomato soup with toast or a bowl of quick-cook noodles boiled with a chicken stock cube, one deseeded, finely sliced chilli, scraps of cooked chicken, coriander leaves and sweet chilli sauce – even better if you can get your hands on a Tom Yum stock cube. Frozen pizza had a few fans, also breakfasty things like eggs and bacon or scrambled eggs with toast. Some just wanted a bowl of cereal. A few adventurous well-prepared souls went for oysters or caviar with champagne. At 4am there are no rules, have whatever you fancy.

THE MINI-BREAK

❦

Your First Weekend Away

*When going away for the weekend with a man, the
woman has her hair done, her bikini-line waxed,
borrows a skirt from her best friend, buys a new
top, dyes her eyelashes, diets, fills fifteen small
plastic containers with lotion, tries on all her
clothes, irons them and packs something 'sexy'.
The man wonders if his wellies are in the car.*

DEBORAH MCKINLAY

How thrilling, your first weekend away! As seen in *Bridget Jones* your first mini-break is desperately exciting but also fraught with possible disasters.

Your destination will dictate the clothes you need to take, but in my experience there are some basics that are essential wherever you go; whether you are fly-fishing in the Scottish

Highlands, spending the weekend at Center Parcs with his kids (it's his weekend to have them and they are just dying to meet you!), going to a fabulous country house hotel or a romantic weekend in Paris at the Georges Cinq.

1. The Little Black Dress (LBD)

Yes, even on the fishing trip. (I am going to totally discount the possibility that you might be camping, that's *not* a mini-break, it's torture.) You will no doubt be staying in a cosy rural pub with an inglenook fireplace and a relaxed, but fabulous, restaurant. The LBD will instantly transform you from fisherman's friend to sexy siren, although less is definitely more so no glitter or feathers. (And not too short, please, these are country folk we are dealing with here.)

At Center Parcs the LBD will be perfect for the Saturday night dinner and dance extravaganza featuring music by Tony Mariano and the Arse-wipes. I don't mean to be denigrating but, really, the first mini-break you go on and he takes his kids. However, it's you that's going out with him, not me, so enjoy!

The LBD is absolutely spot-on attire for the dining room at the country house hotel. I do love these hotels, the big old manor houses set in acres of rambling countryside with their huge drawing rooms stuffed full of commodious sofas, crackling log fires and a never-ending supply of *Country Life* magazines.

I am, of course, especially fond of Sunday morning

breakfast in bed; it has to be the full Monty with cereal, half a grapefruit, poached eggs, crispy bacon, big fat sausages and loads of toast, all eaten whilst reading the Sunday papers and oodles of 'us' time.

The only downside is that they can be just a touch stuffy, can run out of things a bit too often and have a few too many rules.

Here are a few examples of what I mean:

No aperitifs to be taken into the Dining Room.

No smoking (anyone caught smoking will be shot on sight).

No dinner orders taken after 9pm. Kitchen closes at 9.45pm sharp.

The duck's off.

So is the monkfish.

No kippers or vegetarian options are available to those guests who take breakfast in their rooms.

Breakfast orders must be hung on doors by 10pm, sharp.

Board games and magazines are not to be removed from the hall.

Do not remove newspapers from their wooden poles.

We ask our guests to keep all noise to a minimum after 11pm.

Please remove wellies when entering the lobby.

Please vacate allocated parking space by 10am on day of departure.

I can live with these if the hotel is grand enough and in a beautiful and romantic location, but the one thing that I do find hard to swallow is that the wonderful breakfast I described in the previous paragraph is always, without fail, on the glacial side of tepid and it's just not worth the calories.

But everything is forgiven when, upon discovering a hidden window seat in the grand hall overlooking the lawns, I'm served a proper afternoon tea which, by definition, must include cucumber sandwiches (crusts off), warm scones with clotted cream and strawberry jam, tiny éclairs (with coffee icing not chocolate), and a never-ending supply of scalding tea made with leaves, not bags.

For that I'll give up smoking, remove my wellies, forfeit the kippers, even take off my stilettos and walk on tiptoe after 11pm to avoid the clatter of heels on the stone floors. Well, they're the rules, aren't they?

The Georges Cinq, Paris. *Oui, ma chérie*, your LBD will take you anywhere you wish to go. Paris is for lovers, especially well-dressed, sexy little minxes wearing sexy little black dresses.

2. Lingerie

This really needs no explanation, and if it does you don't deserve to be in Pink Cloud. Suffice to say, anything black is sexy and flattering and in the words of the infamous Dorothy Parker, 'brevity is the soul of lingerie'. Buy yourself a basque; it'll do wonders for your waist and his libido. Wear it under your LBD at dinner with stockings and knickers that are both pretty and brief.

3. A Fabulous Peignoir

What is a peignoir? It's French for dressing gown and if it sounds sexier and more glamorous in French than in English, it's because that is precisely what a peignoir or dressing gown is supposed to be, sexy and glamorous. It should NOT, under any circumstances, be some great wad of greying towelling or, worse yet, the monstrosity that is padded, flower-strewn crimplene the colour of cat sick.

Treat yourself; invest in something long and floaty that appears to be fashioned from the wings of butterflies to drape over yourself whilst chilling in your room after a shower, eating breakfast in bed, watching television or before, after or even during sex. A pair of fluffy high-heeled mules wouldn't go amiss either and will drive him mad.

I drink champagne when I'm happy and when I'm sad.
Sometimes I drink it when I'm alone.
When I have company I consider it obligatory.
I trifle with it when I'm not hungry
and drink it when I am.
Otherwise, I never touch it – unless I'm thirsty.

LILY BOLLINGER

4. Champagne

Bring along a couple of bottles of good champagne. He will be flattered; it's so much cheaper than ordering it from room service and you can surprise him over the course of the weekend.

5. Caviar

Pack a small pot of the best caviar you can afford (or if you're not exactly flush some lumpfish roe, which looks exactly like caviar), some Ritz crackers and one lemon. Once again, you're going to surprise him with these over the weekend.

6. A Board Game

Yes, you read it right, I am indeed suggesting that you bring a game with you. Scrabble, backgammon, chess, whatever it is that you enjoy. You won't be in bed all weekend and sitting in the bar of your hotel playing a game over a few drinks is fun and a great way of bonding. It's about finding each other's inner child.

Lastly, don't forget to bring along some really gorgeous-smelling massage oil, a pair of skyscraper heels to go with the LBD, an evening bag, perfume, a sexy nightdress and lots of scented candles and tea lights. Candles really do personalise a hotel room, but please don't forget to blow them out, we want the fire in our loins, not in our room.

*I have found that there ain't no surer way to find
out whether you like people or hate them than
to travel with them.*

MARK TWAIN

Despite good intentions, what starts out as a relaxing break can quickly disintegrate into the weekend from hell through no fault of our own. There are a few things to watch out for.

If you're selecting the destination of your mini-break together, then so much the better. If, on the other hand, one is surprising the other then make sure you are not too extreme. For instance, if you're into gliding and he's scared of heights, a gliding weekend in the Dordogne ain't gonna go down too well. In this case less is definitely more.

The whole point of the exercise is to get away from it all and get to know each other better. The problem is, doing just that can sometimes throw a teeny-weeny spanner in the works.

Up till now you've probably seen one another two or three times a week and are relatively independent of each other, enjoying a voyage of discovery vis-à-vis each other's lifestyles, views, habits and foibles. One of the joys in life is that we are all unique, thus every new relationship brings with it differing perspectives, opposing views and diverse philosophies. It can be a great opportunity to embrace fresh ideals and learn from each other. How fabulous.

Except when we are together for longer periods of time, for example, on our first mini-break. Over a weekend we may find that sometimes, on some things, we clash a little. Remember, it's all part of the journey we're sharing; if all of us held the same beliefs and enjoyed similar things, life would be very boring indeed.

> *My problem is how to reconcile my net*
> *income with my gross habits.*
>
> ERROL FLYNN

In my experience, the two things that most people argue about on holiday are money and trying to agree what to do when they get there.

Let's deal with money first. Not for nothing is it known as the root of all evil.

Money – a simple word of two syllables that is singularly responsible for the premature demise of far too many, otherwise perfectly healthy, fledgling relationships.

Everyone has different ideas on how to spend it and what to spend it on. I confess that I'm a total hedonist (you've probably spotted that) and I am irritatingly free with my cash, especially on holiday. I tend to follow my grandfather's adage, 'better one day as a lion than one hundred as a sheep.' (It sounds rather more poetic in Italian, but you get my drift.)

I personally have a wealth of experience on this particular

stumbling block. Here's a good example of what can go awry on a weekend away with a loved one.

When I'm on holiday you can be sure that, despite breakfast being included in the hotel tariff, the offer of delicious pastries, exotic fruits, Eggs Benedict and some-times even pancakes will leave me cold. Invariably I'll just have coffee. You see, there's nothing I love more after a bit of sightseeing than hunting out a cute little restaurant and partaking of a leisurely and fulsome lunch which allows me to sample the local produce, especially the wine. If I eat breakfast I won't be hungry for lunch, it's totally logical.

Except, this seemingly innocent pleasure drove my ex potty. He couldn't understand the logic of refusing a per-fectly good breakfast that was paid for in favour of a lunch that was not.

You see what I'm getting at? I guess a lot of guys would be less than impressed at my extravagance and those of a more parsimonious nature would, I am quite sure, see it as a waste of money. And do you know what? They'd be right. But it's my mini-break too and I want to enjoy it as much as possible and if that means skipping breakfast in favour of lunch, fine.

So shoot me!

Men are from earth. Women are from earth.
Deal with it.

SLOGAN ON A T-SHIRT

The way we like to spend our leisure time can be another bone of contention. I love going to local food markets and can spend hours mooching around, especially somewhere like France or Italy where the produce is so diverse. I also love wandering through galleries and, of course, being female, I'm passionate about shopping.

The ex also enjoyed doing the markets and shared my passion for food but he truly hated shopping. He also had no interest whatsoever in the arts (philistine), but adored old churches, visiting football stadiums and spending evenings in as many bars as possible, often staying there until dawn.

So, here's the thing. Clearly we liked each other, otherwise we wouldn't have been away together in the first place and, sure, we had our differences, but as I said, if we were all the same life would be pretty dull. So how did we make it work?

We relished our common ground and compromised on our differences, it really was that simple. Sometimes I'd have breakfast with him and in turn the next day he'd skip breakfast and would enjoy lunch, possibly even more than me, or if he accompanied me to a fabulous gallery I in turn escorted him on a magical mystery tour of every bar in town.

One of the most influential and powerful words in the language of love has to be, compromise. It's quite simple, you negotiate until you reach agreement and then you make a plan that ensures each of you is happy and getting what they need. Like I said, it's easy.

> *Get your facts right first then you can*
> *distort them as much as you want.*
>
> MARK TWAIN

So once you iron out the blips you have the makings of a fabulous weekend. But wouldn't it be nice to have some insurance?

What if you had some tricks up your sleeve that guaranteed your man a weekend of such never-to-be-forgotten pleasure that he would come to regard *this* mini-break as a benchmark for all the mini-breaks of his future and of his past.

Before I go on, please refer to the list of essentials at the start of this chapter and have to hand items 4 and 5, plus the massage oil and candles.

Late one afternoon when the two of you are relaxing in your hotel room before going to dinner suggest that you have a bath together. Make it clear that you are going to pamper him for a change. Call room service and ask for a champagne bucket full of ice, two champagne flutes and a sharp knife. Chill one of the bottles of champagne you so cleverly brought with you in the bucket and cut the lemon in half with the sharp knife.

Hotel bathrooms always have lots of bubble bath, so

run a bath using everything you have to hand. Make sure it's neither too hot nor too cold and that it smells divine. Light the candles and tea lights you brought with you and place them around the bath.

Carry the chilled champagne into the bathroom, pop the cork, grab a glass each and jump into the tub together à la Julia Roberts and Richard Gere in *Pretty Woman*. So romantic.

Lie in the bath, sip champagne, whisper sweet nothings and, most importantly, relax.

After your bath give each other massages. Take your time, this is not about the two-minutes-round-the-shoulders rubdowns but, using the massage oil you brought with you, real top-to-toe massages. You'll both be purring like kittens by the end of it and probably have a little snooze.

Now for the pièce de résistance.

When you awake in a loved-up haze and find you are both a little peckish for a pre-dinner hors d'oeuvre, take your Ritz crackers, top them with little caviar and a squeeze of lemon and nibble away contentedly, polishing off the remainder of the champagne and possibly opening another bottle.

If he wasn't in love with you before, he is now.

Love is supreme and unconditional;
Like is nice but limited.

DUKE ELLINGTON

So, you have made it back from your mini-break in one piece and are more into each other than ever. You are tentatively beginning to share a little more of each other's lives and are spending time together during the week after work instead of just at the weekends.

You now have favourite TV shows that you just *have* to watch à deux and are starting to fit into each other's routines, thus establishing your own *shared* routines around them. Weekends are spent mooching around, seeing a movie, shopping, eating out, walking in parks and generally doing all that gorgeous stuff you used to enviously watch other couples enjoying, whilst wondering if it would ever happen to you.

Well, guess what, it has.

You are now in the next stage of Pink Cloud, you're feeling a little less crazy and sleep deprived, but you're still ruled by his pheromones and your passion.

You're beginning to be more open and honest with each other and you no longer feel you always have to be on top form, especially after you've had a bad day and need a large drink and a cuddle.

You are also more relaxed sartorially and don't feel you have to look like you just stepped out of *Vogue* all the time, you're happy to spend the odd evening slouching around with no make-up on in your oldest ripped jeans. (Well, ok then, maybe just a lick of lip gloss, but no trackies please, we're not *that* relaxed and frankly never should be.)

INDOOR PICNICS

Stop the World, I Want to Get Off

Oh, why can't we break from all this, just you and I,
and lodge with my fleas in the hills – I mean flee
to my lodge in the hills.

GROUCHO MARX

 Do you ever have the urge to scream, 'stop the world, I want to get off'? I think that's what our friend Groucho had in mind; taking a weekend away from the world, battening down the hatches, switching off the phones and partaking of some serious R&R. It's the joy of just hanging out together for a whole weekend, doing nothing in particular except eating, drinking, talking, watching TV, making love, reading, going for the odd walk, listening to music or maybe even venturing out to catch a movie. It's the perfect release in those times when you are both weary and in need of some tranquillity, stillness and calm.

And, of course, each other.

Sunday nights are my hunkering down nights. I make a point of locking the front door obscenely early and repeating the mantra: 'Ain't no one going out! Ain't no one coming in!'

Cosy weekends at home are perfect for Indoor Picnics. Whilst I have a weakness for proper sit-down dinners à deux there are times when I want something far less structured, less fancy and, frankly, a lot less hard work, although we do still want to maintain a sense of occasion, the feeling that we have made a bit of an effort.

As usual these things take a little advance planning, but once you've stocked up with the things you need you can spend the rest of the weekend doing absolutely nothing – and the good news is, there's no cooking involved.

My soul is satisfied as with a rich feast.
PSALMS 63.5

On your way home from work on a Friday evening swing past an Italian deli and do some serious shopping, picking up all your favourite gourmet foods. If you are unsure what to get, allow me to suggest 150g (5oz) each of Prosciutto di Parma, salami, mortadella and maybe

Bresaola, although I find the imported stuff a little dry so ask to taste it first.

If meat's not your thing, you could pick up around 200g (7oz) of Italian seafood salad and a selection of cheeses; some Taleggio, a soft cheese from Lombardy, a hunk of Parmigiano, which is hard but wonderfully crumbly when fresh, and if you have never tried it before I urge you to get some Dolcelatte Marscarponato, it's a blue-veined cheese rather like Gorgonzola but layered with mascarpone. It's cheese heaven.

Don't pass by the marinated vegetables; peppers, sun-dried tomatoes, giardiniera (pickled veggies) and mushrooms in olive oil go wonderfully with fresh bread, mustards, pickles and sauces. But don't stop there, get anything else that takes your fancy – remember you're shopping for the whole weekend.

Most good delis now do a few ready-to-eat hot dishes as well as fabulous fresh pasta and ravioli, stock up on these and one of their fresh pasta sauces and, sod it, some of those gorgeous homemade Canoli for pudding. Pad the meals out with a few ripe tomatoes, a good selection of salad leaves, extra virgin oil and some balsamic vinegar.

Of course, last but not least, don't forget a couple of bottles of Prosecco (sparkling Italian wine) and a couple of bottles of decent red.

Once you've managed to carry it all home in the manner of a small donkey and unpacked it all, your work is done. I suggest you reward yourself with a long, hot bath, slather your body in your expensive body oil and change into your most comfy 'lounging around clothes'. By definition these are not the sexiest items in your wardrobe, but, I reiterate, please avoid tracksuit bottoms. Candy-stripe pink pyjama bottoms with a white vest top or, better yet, an oversize man's shirt with a pair of boxer shorts is a much better look.

Once you're both in situ with the doors bolted and all communication with the outside world has ceased, spread a picnic rug on the floor of your living room and cover it with a tablecloth. Lay out all of your goodies exactly as if you were having a picnic outdoors, turn down the lights, grab some candles, pop the cork on the now-chilled Prosecco, put on some mellow music and sit cross-legged on the floor ready to graze on your easily-assembled, lavish and truly magnificent feast.

I bet you're already feeling better and just a little mischievous and childlike; picnics seem to have that effect on people.

If you really want to get into character, in the background you could play DVDs of fields, beaches and forests or, if you're feeling especially amorous, images of a log fire complete with crackling sound effects are supposed to work every time!

MEET ME AFTER WORK AND BRING A TOOTHBRUSH

Midweek Suppers

When you go to work, if your name is on the building you're rich. If your name is on your desk you're middle class. And if your name is on your shirt, you're poor.

RICH HALL

Things are going really well, it's been about 3 months since you first met and you are starting to see a lot more of each other midweek, spending odd nights at one or the other's home.

Time for a note of caution. It's a lot easier for him to come to your place after work than for you to go to his. All he requires for the next day is a change of underwear, a fresh shirt, toothbrush and razor and that's it, he's good to go. As any woman will tell you it takes a lot more than a quick splash of water and a toothbrush before we can face our public.

We women require a small skip-ful of absolute essentials; make-up remover, a night-time facial moisturiser, a body moisturiser, shampoo, conditioner, leave-in conditioner, day-time moisturiser, *all* our make-up, tweezers, hairdryer, hair-straighteners, brushes, a whole new outfit with accessories, tights, underwear, a change of shoes, perfume, the toothbrush and the huge black bag we lug it all around in.

You can always spot the regular midweek sleepover babes, they're the ones with the huge black bag slung over one shoulder who walk with a slight stoop, albeit with a glint in their eye.

No one wants to eat out every night and, let's face it, takeaways can get a little tiring. There are those evenings when you both walk through the door somewhat frazzled and want nothing more than to chill out on the sofa with some good but simple food, a glass of wine and watch *EastEnders* followed by, bubblegum for the brain, a reality TV show.

> *I'm dating a homeless woman. It's easy*
> *to talk her into staying over.*
> GARRY SHANDLING

Here are a few after-work suppers that are easy to shop for and require very little effort, which is exactly what you need after a hard day's work. With a nod to healthy eating we really only need one course on a school night, so I haven't bothered with a pudding as fresh fruit will suffice.

It's nice to cook together, both doing your bit towards preparing supper, working side by side, glass of wine in hand with perhaps some music playing in the background whilst you unwind and swap stories about your respective days, stopping every now and then for a kiss.

Pan-fried Salmon Niçoise (ready in 20 mins)

2 salmon fillets (preferably wild); 350g (12oz) new potatoes, boiled until tender and halved; 200g (7oz) green beans, steamed al dente (keep both warm); 6 black olives; 8 cherry tomatoes, halved; 2 boiled eggs, quartered; 4 anchovy fillets.

For the dressing: 4 tbsp olive oil; 2 tsp Dijon mustard; 1 tsp brown sugar; 2 tbsp lemon juice; freshly ground salt and pepper.

Combine all the ingredients for the dressing, including a good grind of salt and pepper, whisk and leave to infuse. Flash fry the salmon fillets in a splash of olive oil for about a minute on each side (thus leaving them a little pink in the middle). Take care not to break the fillets up, then add another tablespoon of olive oil to the pan together with the potatoes, green beans, tomato halves and olives and sauté until warmed. Divide the vegetables between two plates, place the salmon on top followed by the anchovies and quarters of boiled egg, drizzle dressing over the whole thing and serve with some warm crusty bread and a nice, chilled white wine.

How easy is that?

Chicken with Goat's Cheese and Roasted Vegetables

2 boneless chicken breasts; 1 medium red onion, cut into wedges; around 20 largish cherry tomatoes, kept whole; 1 sweet potato in 1in dice; 1 red pepper cut into 2in squares, not strips; 100g (4oz) soft goat's cheese; 1 tbsp fresh tarragon leaves; 2 cloves of garlic, finely chopped; olive oil; 1 tbsp milk, freshly ground salt and pepper.

You will also need cocktail sticks for securing the chicken breasts.

Heat the oven to 200°C (400°F). Coat the vegetables with a couple of glugs of olive oil combined with the chopped garlic and place in a shallow, ovenproof casserole dish. Mash the cheese together with the milk and tarragon, then slip your fingers under the skin of each chicken breast to form a pocket and stuff with the cheese mixture, distributing it evenly along the breast. Season well with salt and pepper and secure skin with cocktail sticks to ensure no cheese can seep out during cooking.

Sit the chicken on the vegetables, drizzle with olive oil and cook for 30–40 minutes until chicken is cooked, skin is crispy and golden and it is oozing melted cheese. Once the chicken is out of the oven, remove the cocktail sticks.

Serve with a nice Shiraz and maybe a green leaf salad dressed with the chicken juices and a squeeze of lemon juice.

It has been noted that there are more carnivorous menus in *Eat Me* than there are vegetarian. (I'm talking about real vegetarians here, the ones who eat no meat, no fish, no fowl; those sensitive souls who won't eat anything with a face. Although I remain mystified at how they resist the gravity-defying pull of a bacon sandwich.)

Well, here is a dish that will satisfy both vegetarians and even the most committed carnivores. It comes from one of my favourite restaurants in the world, Original Sin in Singapore, which, despite being evangelically vegetarian, serves dishes of such gratifying complexity that even the most ardent meat eaters flock to its doors.

Risotto with Taleggio and Pumpkin

I never really understood the point of risotto until I tasted it at Grissini in Hong Kong, it was stunning and once the chef taught me how to make it properly and I started to cook it myself I became utterly hooked. It's all about timing, you can't rush a risotto.

Having said that, people are under the misconception that it's labour intensive and temperamental. Poppycock, all you need is a litre of hot stock (if I'm in a hurry I will happily use Marigold Vegetable Stock or Kallo Organic Chicken Stock cubes); 1 medium chopped onion; 40g (1½oz) butter; 2 handfuls of arborio or other risotto rice per person; a small glass of white wine; 3 handfuls of cooked pumpkin, cut into ½ in dice; 50g (2oz) Taleggio cheese, cut up into cubes; and freshly ground salt and pepper.

Heat the stock and keep it simmering on the back burner in a heavy pan on a lowish heat. Sauté your onion until very soft, add the rice and stir, ensuring each grain is covered in butter, then, turning up the heat slightly, add the wine and allow it to reduce by half, stirring constantly. Pour in a ladleful of stock, let it come to the boil then keep it at a bubbling simmer, adding ladle after ladle of stock and stirring all the time for 20 minutes. As the rice absorbs the stock it will become soft and plump.

At this point add the chopped pumpkin and another ladle of stock, stirring all the time. Now taste to see if the rice is cooked – I like mine quite soft, although it's fashionable to eat it al dente with a bit of bite left in the grain. Now check the seasoning and add the cubes of Taleggio, gently folding them into the rice until they start to melt. The risotto should be a little soupy but not too liquid, if it's too dry add a touch more stock.

Serve immediately with a large green salad and a crisp Sauvignon Blanc.

My grandmother was famous for her Risotto alla Milanese and had an old saying, '*Il riso nasce nel acqua e muore nel vino.*' This is literally translated as 'rice is born in water and should die in wine', which basically means that one should never even consider making a risotto without the addition of a glass of wine. I had to smile recently when a very famous TV chef did just that, my grandmother must have turned in her grave.

RUDE FOOD

❦

It's Playtime

*Erotic is when you use a feather,
kinky is when you use the whole chicken.*

ANON

I tried to resist, I really did, but my work here would not be complete if I didn't include at least a page on Rude Food whilst we are in Pink Cloud. For the sake of propriety, I won't go into too much detail (what you do with this lot is up to you), but I can't resist giving you a list of ingredients that could make for a very amusing and titillating evening.

One blindfold
Runny honey

Fresh strawberries
Chocolate ice-cream
Tabasco sauce
Whipped cream
Ice cubes
Melted chocolate, preferably still warm
Champagne
Orange jelly

Do you remember the fridge scene in *9½ Weeks* where Kim Basinger is sat on the floor in the half-light, next to an open fridge, blindfolded, and Mickey Rourke starts to feed her morsels of food? A strawberry, some chocolate cake, a tiny amount of Tabasco on whipped cream, ice cubes, honey squirted into her mouth and dribbling down her chin . . .

You get the picture.

The game becomes increasingly feverish and they both end up covered in chocolate, cream, honey and anything else they had to hand. Naughty. Very naughty. Well, that's pretty much what I have in mind here.

THOSE THREE LITTLE WORDS

※

He Loves Me. He Loves Me Not.

Love is an irresistible desire to be irresistibly desired.
ROBERT FROST

 So it feels like it may be time to utter those three little words, huh?

You know exactly which three words I'm talking about; it's been in the air for a while now and whilst you have come very close, neither of you has actually *said* 'it' and you don't want to be the first one to do so. You both know it's there just waiting to pop out and, sometimes, you find yourself biting your lip to stop yourself from saying it. Then, out of the blue, along comes that moment where you just can't hold it in any longer – it's as if you have Tourette's for lovers.

I LOVE YOU
I LOVE YOU
I LOVE YOU
I LOVE YOU
I LOVE YOU
I LOVE YOU

I LOVE YOU.

You can't believe anything this incredible could happen to *you* and are sure that no one has ever felt like this before. But the amazing thing is that you both feel it, you both 'I love you' each other . . . Finally, 'love' isn't one-sided or unrequited.

It's a miracle, it's mind-blowing and, best of all, it's yours, all yours!

Now things are really hotting up, you look back on the dark and gloomy days before you met in total wonderment, how could you ever have thought you were happy? How could you have doubted that you would one day meet 'the one'? How did you ever live without each other?

Now everything is done together. You maintain separate apartments, even though you spend five nights out of seven at his place, and you now take for granted that holidays will be taken together. Everything in the garden is rosy, rosy, rosy.

Or is it?

YOUR FIRST QUARREL

The Agony and the Ecstasy

Oh innocent victims of Cupid
remember this terse little verse,
to let a fool kiss you is stupid
to let a kiss fool you is worse.

E. Y. HARBURG

 Oh dear!

You've just had your first big, ghastly, nasty, noisy, proper row.

Generally, first rows blow up over silly little things: who said what to whom, what they really meant by it, why they said it in the first place, blah, blah, blah, amid lots of door slamming and sobbing (her), huffing, puffing and leaving (him). Blah, blah, blah . . .

Someone feels slighted and someone feels hurt, the problem is the pair of you have been on your best behaviour since the day you met and have perhaps not been entirely yourselves. All perfectly normal behaviour for Pink Cloud, of course, but when you do have your first disagreement and revert to type everything tends to get blown out of all proportion.

The big problem is that you have no history of resolving any arguments to refer to so therefore you both over-react, driven by the fear of losing each other but unable to call a halt as you don't know each other well enough yet to know how. Fear can make us act even against our own best interests, ostensibly cutting off our noses to spite our faces.

A first row can rarely be avoided; there comes a time in all relationships when our true selves come to light. We can only pretend to be perfect for so long. We meet as strangers, two people who thus far have lived totally separate lives with totally different backgrounds so it would be a bloody miracle if we agreed on everything. Not to mention bloody boring.

So what do we do? Where do we go from here? How do we get back to our fluffy pink cloud?

I believe that a little time and space solves most petty arguments and this type of squabble, no matter how heated or vitriolic it becomes, falls slap bang into that category. When this happens to me I tend to hole up in my apartment

for a couple of days and lay low, thus giving things a
to calm down. It's the sensible and mature thing to ___.

Except, there's one problem, when I'm aggrieved I am
neither sensible nor mature. I stay mad for a while then
move on to indignant, swiftly followed by sad after a bout
of listening to what I refer to as 'self-harm music' or, 'music
to slash your wrists by'; David Gray, Dido, Jeff Buckley and
anything by Leonard Cohen works every time.

I know that lots of women lose their appetites in a
crisis, but I'm afraid I'm not one of them. When I'm angry
and upset I cook for myself as if I were cooking for
someone very special which, of course, I am. (Even if *he*
doesn't think so right now!)

I know exactly what I want on an occasion such as this.
I want something I can really get my teeth into, something
to get my jaws gnashing, a dish that is universally trashy
but, if done correctly, utterly divine – the humble hamburger. But this is not just any burger picked up on the
high street, I'm talking about one of my homemade, chargrilled, bacon cheeseburgers with chunky fries, ketchup
and a green leaf salad, all washed down with a diet coke.

Something to Chew on . . .

200g (7oz) lean minced beef; 1 small onion, finely chopped;
1 tbsp olive oil; freshly ground salt and pepper; 1 slice of
mature cheddar cheese; 2 slices of back bacon, cooked until
crispy; 1 hamburger bun, toasted only on the cut side.

To serve: A portion of oven-cooked chunky fries; 2 handfuls mixed leaves dressed with balsamic and olive oil; and lots of ketchup and mustard, if you like it.

Gently sauté the onion in a frying pan until soft, let it cool and then combine it with the meat. Season the meat mixture with salt and pepper and roll it into a ball to make a burger around 2cm (¾in) thick.

Making sure all the other components are ready, the fries, bacon and salad leaves, brush the burger with a little oil and cook under a very hot grill for about 5 minutes on each side, depending on how you like it. At the last minute put a slice of cheese over the top of the meat and allow it to melt slightly.

Serve in the toasted bun and top with the grilled bacon and ketchup.

It works for me.

(I don't eat a great deal of red meat but I do find that anger and upset causes me to crave exactly that. Those of you who prefer to abstain can get pretty much the same satisfaction by replacing the minced steak with chicken, fish or, for true veggies, a grilled portobello mushroom.)

Anyway, now we've eaten and are feeling better, but a little lonely . . . how do we get back to Pink Cloud?

In my experience, no one is ever totally right and no one is ever completely wrong. It takes two to tango and you can tango right back into each other's arms with a simple, 'I'm sorry' and either compromise on what you argued about, or agree to disagree. Just as it takes two people to start an argument, it takes two people to end one.

However, to help the path of true love run that little bit smoother I've come up with some suggestions for a Kiss and Make Up menu for when the storm has subsided and the sun has once again got his hat on.

Now's the time to prepare a romantic dinner together safe in the knowledge that your first row, whilst horrid, is over and you came out the other side a little stronger and knowing each other a little better. Disagreements have a strange way of clearing the air and bringing us closer as we learn about each other.

Steamed Tiger Prawns with Aïoli

A simple but luxurious starter, but to make it more simple you can cheat with the aïoli and add some finely chopped garlic, a little mustard and a squeeze of lemon to a jar of good-quality mayonnaise.

The Prawns:

Buy about 14–20 medium-sized raw tiger prawns (depending on their size) and place them in a colander with half a lemon over a pan of boiling water. Steam them until they turn pink, about 3 or 4 minutes. Set them aside to cool.

The Aïoli:

½ a clove of garlic, peeled; 1 tsp salt; 1 small egg yolk; ½ tsp Dijon mustard; 285ml (½ pint) extra virgin olive oil; lemon juice to taste.

Combine the salt and garlic with a pestle and mortar until they form a paste. (If you do not have a pestle and mortar, crush your garlic on a chopping board and combine with the salt using a palette knife.) Place the egg yolk and the mustard in a bowl and whisk, then slowly start to add the olive oil in small quantities whisking all the time, you can add larger amounts towards the end. When you have a thick wobbly mayonnaise, you can add the garlic and lemon juice (to taste), whisking with each addition. Season to taste, chill, then serve with the prawns and perhaps some small bits of toasted baguette.

Alex's Special Breasts

We are, of course, talking chicken here. Every woman I know has one foolproof dish that she just knows is going to work for her every time. This is mine, you can adopt it and tinker with it as you wish. It has had many incarnations but this is the original and probably the best.

Once again, I urge you to buy your chicken breasts from a proper butcher's shop as the ones you buy in the supermarket generally no longer have the fillets attached.

2 x 200g (7oz) skinless chicken breasts with fillet intact; 1 pack 80g (3oz) Boursin cheese; 4 sun-dried tomatoes in olive oil, drained and roughly chopped; 2 tbsp fresh parsley, finely chopped; 2 large slices Parma ham; a pack of ready-rolled puff pastry; 1 egg, beaten; sea salt and freshly ground black pepper to taste.

Preheat the oven to 200°C (400°F). In a bowl, combine the Boursin, sun-dried tomatoes and parsley to make a smooth but firm paste, if it's a bit stiff add a splash of water and mix until smooth.

Pull back the chicken fillet to create a pocket by cutting into the underside of the breast, then push in as much of the cheese and sun-dried tomato mixture as will comfortably fit, pulling the fillet back into place to close it and then wrapping the breasts in the Parma ham. Then, as if you were applying a bandage, cut the ready-rolled pastry into 8 strips about 20cm (8in) long and 5cm (2in) wide and wrap them around the chicken breasts, starting at one end and working your way up to the other. (This sounds incredibly complicated but really it isn't, it's just hard to explain.) Brush the chicken parcels with a little egg and cook in the preheated oven for 30 minutes. Serve with a watercress and avocado salad dressed with olive oil, a spoon of wholegrain mustard and a squeeze of lemon juice.

Nonno's Ice-cream

I wouldn't imagine either of you are now hungry enough or can be bothered to make a proper dessert, so here's another tip from my grandfather. It tastes gorgeous and couldn't be simpler.

Top some vanilla ice-cream with crushed rataffia biscuits, or whatever biscuits you have, then add a large jigger of your favourite liqueur that has been warmed in a metal ladle over a gas flame. Voilà!

PLAYLIST

Marvin Gaye: **Let's Get it On**
Liberty X: **Just a Little**
INXS: **Need You Tonight**
Andy Williams: **Can't Take My Eyes off of You**
Roberta Flack: **First Time Ever I Saw Your Face**
Mis-Teeq: **Scandalous**
Katie Melua: **Closest Thing to Crazy**
Etta James: **Just Want to Make Love to You**
Barry White: **My First, My Last, My Everything**
Chaka Khan and Rufus: **Ain't Nobody**

THE END OF THE BEGINNING

We are about to leave The Beginning and head for the new and uncharted territory of The Middle. Please don't feel you're leaving something behind because you will be gaining so much more than you could ever imagine.

THE MIDDLE

Wherever so she was, there was Eden.

MARK TWAIN

Eat, friends, drink and be drunk with love.

SONG OF SOLOMON 5.1

CONGRATULATIONS!

You have made it to the start of The Middle (or is that the beginning of The End?).

THE MIDDLE WELCOMES ONE AND ALL
You are cordially invited to:

Sunday Luncheons, Midweek Suppers,
Summer Picnics, Mother's Day Lunch,
Xmas Day Extravaganzas, Guy Fawkes BBQs,
Birthday Parties, Sunday Brunches, High Teas,
Dinner Parties for 12, New Year's Eve Suppers

The possibilities are endless, your togetherness brings with it a generosity of spirit (and the need to show off a little).

Then, of course, there's cooking simply to please one another:

Breakfast in Bed, Summer Picnics,
Intimate Dinner for Two, By Invitation Only,
Celebration Dinner for the Good Days,
Comfort Tucker for the Not-So-Good Days.

Feeding and nurturing the one you love is such a joy. Of course, at this point a dishwasher is paramount . . .

It's time to celebrate, throw open the windows, let the sunshine in and the good times roll; *we are in love* and we want to share our (sometimes nauseating) happiness with the whole wide world.

At this stage the two of you are quite convinced that you actually invented love. You are both utterly confident that no other lovers could have ever felt the same way. You believe, quite sincerely, that you have perfected the art of fornication and you just can't get enough of each other (you, of course, call it Making Love).

You endlessly delight in recounting to anyone who will listen how you two lovebirds met, rejoicing in the minuti-ae of 'that special moment'. Your friends have become mere extras with ears in the miraculous and joyous phenomenon that is your love affair.

You start doing the 'joined at the hip' thing, socialising almost exclusively with other couples, basking in each other's, oh-so-perfect, loved-up company. You exist in a collective consciousness where two rule the world and love is a many splendour'd thing!

N.B. Don't even begin to tell me you cannot empathise with the above, we've ALL been there and boy, oh boy, does *lurve* feel good when you're in it!

7TH HEAVEN

֍

Two Become One

*She hath my mind so displaced I
shall never find my home.*

ANDREW MARVELL

These days you are very much a team. All invitations are now jointly received, you get post at each other's houses and, as if more proof of 'coupledom' was required, you are both on each other's 'in case of emergency' numbers at work. You now spend practically every night together and on the odd occasion you do not it would be unthinkable if you didn't call each other at least two or three times over the course of the day.

You are now referred to by others in that sing-song, one-name manner that occurs when two people have been together a while Mickey&Minnie, Homer&Marge, Richard&Judy, Tom&Jerry and, well, you get the idea; two names become one.

All of this indicates that you have now moved on from the giddy, thrilling, though sometimes-uncertain, phase of Pink Cloud to the cocoon of wellbeing and security that is 7th Heaven. Your relationship is rock solid and now is a time of consolidation and the melding of two lives into one.

Breathless anticipation is replaced by languid desire, passion is driven by the stability of love rather than the fear of loss and you are both beginning to feel the time has come where living together just feels right. As Woody Allen put it, 'Love is like a shark, if it doesn't move forward it dies.'

From a purely practical perspective, after a while the day-to-day grind of shunting between two different addresses tends to wear down even the most ardent of lovers. (Especially we girls, given the sheer volume of kit we need to haul around with us in a bid to look good, and anyway, what's the point of paying two lots of out-goings if you spend pretty much every night of the week together?)

Home is where the mortgage is.

BILLY CONNOLLY

The practicalities of moving in together and sharing a home are numerous but it is the romantic incentives that, for two people who cannot bear to be parted even for one night, truly compel us to want to live together. Practicalities be damned, they wouldn't get a look in if we were not just plumb crazy about each other.

Setting up home together generally means pooling your resources and acquiring a house that you wouldn't possibly have been able to afford on your own. This is one of the many advantages of living à deux, and there is something magical about fixing up your first house together. Choosing the colours, décor and furniture that reflect both of your styles is an important step in your relationship; it's an amazing feeling to know that together you can transform this house into a home, a haven of love and tranquillity which projects a tangible display of the bond that you have forged.

You have now arrived in the land of shared everything: Sunday morning cuddles, takeaways and TV, joint gas bills, dirty socks, in-laws, out-laws, cold feet on warm backs, someone to share the good and bad days with, somebody to take things out on, to put you to bed when you're drunk, scratch your back, tell you your bum does *not* look fat in that, somebody to blame when everything goes wrong and who will praise you when it doesn't.

Two become one. Good luck!

However, be warned, the day you actually move in can

be somewhat fraught and by the end of it you will both be totally knackered. But when the removal men have gone and the two of you stop, look around and realise with happy hearts that you've taken the first step towards the rest of your lives together, the tiredness melts away and is replaced by exhilaration. With your arms wrapped around each other you can take a quiet moment to enjoy the calm and the silence of your new home.

Except it's not silent; there's a distinct gurgling sound and it's getting louder and louder . . . The sound of tummies rumbling. Yours.

You suddenly realise you haven't eaten all day and are both absolutely starving, but most of the kitchen is still in boxes and even if it wasn't you have neither the energy nor the inclination to start cooking.

The first evening you spend in your new home is a truly special occasion. I *have* been known to cook on nights such as this, but I don't recommend it unless you have a mother like mine who turns up with an entire dinner consisting of melon and prosciutto, fillet steak with garlic potatoes and salad, plus a fruit salad to finish it off. She produced all of this from the boot of my father's car (along with candles and wine), and then got on with laying the table whilst my dad dealt with the serious matter of unblocking the drains. When everything was done to their satisfaction they left us to enjoy our first dinner in our new home. Thanks, guys.

If you don't have a fairy godmother there's only one thing for it: a celebratory bottle of champagne with a candlelit takeaway. Try and make it as nice as possible: find some plates, glasses, a tablecloth and cutlery and if your table isn't set up yet put a sheet on the floor picnic-style, find some CDs, toast each other and your lovely new home and relish every moment of this magical night.

Love is a mutual understanding.
OSCAR WILDE

A by-product of The Middle is that the inamorati require an audience in which to bask. You want to introduce your new love to everyone: friends, family, acquaintances, your chiropractor, spiritual advisor, to hell with it, even your exes, it's that glorious time when you look at each other in wonder and are desperate to open your home and fridge in a frenzy of blissed-out domesticity.

We are about to wave goodbye to that period of hormonally-charged delirium when food was nibbled on to fuel yet another marathon session between the sheets, rather than to nourish our bodies, and the days when we survived purely on lust and endorphins.

Instead, say hello to and embrace The Middle, where food takes on new meaning. It is at this juncture that we meet each other's families and friends (indulgent smiles all round) and we start to get hungry. The need for razor-sharp hipbones has subsided, sod that, I'm starving, what do you fancy? Let's eat.

We therefore come out of the bedroom and into the dining room. We start to socialise again. We seek the approval of friends and family. We want to show the world we are a couple. Suddenly food is very, very important. We cook for everybody; showing off our new shared home, starry eyes, trendy (and not-so-trendy-but-terribly-clever) friends, designer dinner plates, espresso machine and fusion cooking. Everything is done together, even supermarket shopping is fun, and menus are meticulously planned. We cook together – bonhomie rules.

Store Cupboard Essentials

A man in the home is worth two in the street.
MAE WEST

One of the good things about moving home is that it gives us the opportunity to have a really good clear out and get rid of all our clutter.

I am pretty sure that we've all got a murky kitchen cupboard where long-forgotten and of out-of-date herbs go to die, not to mention those must-have holiday purchases: little bottles of peculiar condiments that tasted wonderfully exotic in a beachfront candlelit restaurant with sand between our toes, but whose distinctive flavour didn't travel too well and are now simply gathering dust. It's time to throw them all out and start again. Dried herbs lose their flavour after being open for three months anyway, so get rid of them.

Here's my list of *my* larder essentials; these are the basics and will ensure that you always have the makings of a really nice dinner without having to rush to the shops.

Oils: extra virgin olive oil for salad dressings, olive oil for cooking and marinading, sunflower oil for frying.

Vinegars: balsamic vinegar and white wine vinegar for dressings, malt vinegar for pouring over chips.

Herbs and spices: Maldon sea salt for the table and for cooking, peppercorns, dried rosemary, whole nutmeg, mixed Provençal herbs, bay leaves, dried whole chillies, dried porcini mushrooms, curry powder, fresh garlic, fresh ginger.

Stock cubes: Kallo organic chicken stock cubes, Marigold Swiss Vegetable Bouillon powder. (Both of these are additive- and MSG-free.)

Pulses: dried cannellini beans, dried chickpeas, dried kidney beans.

Tinned foods: baked beans, Italian tomatoes, tomato purée, coconut milk, sweetcorn, tuna in spring water or olive oil, anchovies in olive oil, olives, peaches in natural juice, Morello cherries, Bird's Custard.

Condiments: Heinz tomato ketchup, Colman's English

mustard, Dijon mustard, Hellmann's mayonnaise, Branston pickle, horseradish sauce, Kikkoman soy sauce, sweet chilli sauce, HP brown sauce, Worcestershire sauce, Tabasco, a small jar of imported, Italian, ready-made pasta sauce for emergencies.

Dried goods: pasta – durum wheat, De Cecco or Barilla spaghetti No.5, penne, tagliatelle verdi; rice – basmati, jasmine, arborio; egg noodles; breakfast cereal.

Baking goods: plain flour, baking powder, cornflour, caster sugar, muscovado sugar, cooking chocolate (70 per cent cocoa solids), vanilla pods, mixed dried fruit.

Tea and coffee: Yorkshire tea bags, 1 jar good-quality instant coffee, vacuum-packed Illy ground coffee, Cadburys drinking chocolate, pack of assorted herbal teas.

Freezer: petit pois, thin-cut chips, 450g (1lb) minced steak, 1 free-range chicken, 1 pack dry-cured back bacon, freshly-grated Parmesan in an airtight container.

This list covers the basics, but you can never have enough fresh herbs; store basil, coriander, parsley, thyme, sage, chives, mint and rosemary in the fridge in airtight containers.

YOU ARE CORDIALLY
INVITED TO . . .

Time to Celebrate

*Nothing is more irritating than not being invited to
a party you wouldn't be caught dead at.*

BILL VAUGHN

In these freethinking, liberal times setting up home together is a contemporary statement of commitment, much as marriage used to be. Whilst I don't think that cohabitation has replaced marriage it has, without doubt, become the norm to live together as an interim step; a sort of 'suck it and see' preamble to the real thing.

Even though living together may feel like less of a commitment than getting married, in reality it's pretty much the same; you are choosing to share a home with a view to spending the rest of your lives together. All that's missing is the piece of paper.

Wait a minute! There's something else missing – a big party and lots of presents. No one would dream of getting married without a bit of a shindig and if moving in together is the preamble to marriage that we have agreed it is, if the shared front door is actually an overture to the diamond solitaire followed by the ubiquitous gold band and Forsaking All Others, Amen, then surely we should be marking the occasion with a celebration of some kind? Some way to commemorate our new life together, something between a housewarming and a wedding reception – but without the vicar or the white dress.

(This menu would also be perfect for an engagement party, should he have sprung for the ring.)

> *Dancing is a perpendicular expression of*
> *a horizontal desire.*
>
> GEORGE BERNARD SHAW

Really good parties require groundwork and a bit of preparation and even though it's all relatively painless, you'll probably need some help. So instead of asking your friends and family to be bridesmaids and ushers as you would for a wedding, ask them to help out. As long as you keep the wine flowing they'll be more than happy to do so.

Schedule the party for a Saturday night, thereby giving you the whole day to get ready. Send out invitations at least a month in advance and don't forget to tell people the reason for the festivities.

Decorate the house with flowers, balloons and anything else you fancy. It's a good idea to get a DJ so you don't have to worry about the music and as it's a celebration of love, get him to play 'your song' so you can have a romantic smooch.

With regards the food, I guess it depends on the number of people you have coming but I'm going to guess at an average of 50 or so. I think a buffet is always a good idea as it can be prepared and laid out prior to the party and your guests can help themselves.

So here's an outline for a lavish celebration buffet. Feel free to adapt it as you wish, it's tough to determine exact quantities but as a rule of thumb I tend to veer towards over- rather than under-catering. The leftovers come in very useful the next day to feed and encourage those lovely people who have offered to help with the cleaning up.

N.B. There's only one thing worse than running out of food and that's running out of booze. Talking of which, it is perfectly acceptable to ask all of your guests to bring a bottle of wine.

One tequila, two tequila, three tequila, floor.
BUDDY SHIRT

I adhere to the beer, wine and soft drinks rule at my parties, a full bar means just that and along with all the mixers it is simply too much like hard work. However, I always prepare one special concoction to get the party off with a bang: my signature cocktail is a Margarita; not for nutin' am I known as the Margarita Queen.

Watermelon Margarita

This luscious blend of watermelon and tequila tastes innocuous, but don't be fooled.

> Makes 50
> 6kg (13lb) chopped watermelon flesh, seedless or with seeds removed and liquidised to give about 4 litres; the juice of 10 limes; 1½ litres (2½ pints) tequila; salt; wedges of watermelon and lime to garnish; bags and bags of ice.

Juice the watermelon and limes on the morning of the party and keep somewhere cool. Pour the liquidised watermelon, lime juice and tequila into a large container; I have a washing-up bowl I keep specifically for mixing cocktails and punches for parties. (I have a wonderful childhood memory of my father making punch for my parents' annual Christmas-morning drinks party. He would mix it and serve it in a rather posh china chamber pot – a gazunda so named because it gazunda the bed – with a great big tinsel bow round it. It never failed to raise a smile.)

As your guests arrive, start making batches of Margarita. Half-fill a blender with ice, top with the watermelon/tequila mix and blend until smooth. Serve in whisky tumblers or small wine glasses. (You could salt the rim of the glasses but I find a lot of people don't like the taste and it's a painstaking process best avoided for these numbers.)

It's a good idea to assign one of your helpers the task of keeping the cocktails coming for an hour or so: everybody should have at least one. Late stragglers will, I'm afraid, just miss out.

You could spend hours preparing canapés and intricate amuse-bouches to go with the Margaritas, but if I'm catering for this many people and there's a sumptuous buffet later, I don't bother. Instead, I keep it simple and scatter platters of nibbles around: grissini, the Italian bread sticks, are great wrapped in finely sliced Parma ham; wrap the ham around the bread stick at an angle from the middle to the top. Crudités always go down well, cut peppers, radishes, fennel, celery, carrots, courgettes, cucumber, and in fact any vegetable you want, into the same-size strips. Lay out some tortilla chips and a bowl of hummus to dip them all in.

Hummus Bi Tahina

500g (1lb 2oz) chickpeas; 5 cloves garlic; 5 tbsp extra virgin olive oil; 500ml (18fl oz) tahina paste; juice of 4 lemons; cayenne pepper; salt.

In a heavy-bottomed saucepan cover the chickpeas with boiling water and soak overnight. Next day bring to the boil and simmer gently for 2 hours until tender. Place in a blender with all the other ingredients apart from cayenne pepper and blend until smooth. Season with salt and cayenne pepper. Serve in glass bowls with a sprinkling of cayenne pepper and a drizzle of olive oil.

Red Pepper, Chilli and Coriander Salsa

6 large red peppers; 6 large red chillies, deseeded and finely chopped (if they are really hot, use less); 2 red onions, finely chopped; 300ml (10fl oz) olive oil; 6 tbsp lemon juice; 2 tbsp brown sugar; 2 handfuls coriander, finely chopped; 2 handfuls parsley, finely chopped; salt and freshly ground black pepper.

Grill the red peppers until their skin is blackened, place in bowl and cover with cling film for 5 minutes. Skin, deseed and finely chop. Mix all the ingredients together with a good grinding of salt and pepper and let the flavours infuse overnight.

I also have a real thing about serving sausages on sticks, I love 'em and so, it seems, does everybody else as they usually disappear faster than I can make them.

CELEBRATION BUFFET

A basket of assorted fresh breads

COLD

Chicken Liver Parfait

White Bean and Tuna Salad

Mozzarella and Tomato Salad with Pesto

*Gammon in Cider with a Mustard and
Caramelised Apple Crust*

*Lemon Roasted Chicken with
Garlic and Rosemary*

*Smoked Salmon Ceviche with Wasabi,
Honey and Lime*

*Oven-baked Mediterranean Vegetables with Balsamic
and Muscovado Sugar*

New Potato and Spring Onion Salad

Mixed Leaf Salad

HOT

Penne con Salsicce al forno

This menu may look like hard work, but with a few people helping it really isn't that bad. A lot of it can be prepared in advance, so provided you are organised it should be pretty painless.

Bread

I wouldn't dream of suggesting you make your own bread but it's a good idea to get lots of different breads with a variety of textures, colours and shapes; such as baguettes, poppy seed and sunflower seed rolls, olive bread, foccacia, ciabatta and some good, hearty wholemeal. A rustic basket piled high looks great on the table.

Chicken Liver Parfait

Easy and quick to prepare, you can make it a couple of days ahead of the party and pop it in the fridge. Please make sure you buy super-fresh livers that are plump and firm to the touch.

500g (1lb 2oz) chicken livers; 3 onions, finely chopped; 6 garlic cloves, finely chopped; milk; 2 glugs olive oil; 1kg (2lb 4oz) unsalted butter; 3 tsp fresh thyme leaves; 200ml (7fl oz) brandy; a dozen fresh sage leaves to decorate.

Place the livers in a shallow dish, pour over enough cold milk to cover them completely, leave them to soak for an hour then drain well. Trim each one carefully to remove any sinews and place on kitchen roll to dry. Fry the onion and garlic in olive oil on a low to medium heat until soft. Melt the butter over a low heat and drain off the fat leaving the milky residue behind in the pan. Keep the butter somewhere warm.

Heat some olive oil in a large, heavy-bottomed pan and add the thyme. Fry the livers in batches for 1 minute on each side until cooked on the outside and pink in the middle. Add the brandy to the pan with the last batch, let it sizzle for a few seconds then pour it, plus all the livers, into a blender along with three-quarters of the melted butter, cooked onions and garlic. Whizz until totally smooth. (You may have to do this in batches.)

To finish off, push the mixture through a fine sieve with a spatula. Season the parfait with freshly ground salt, pepper and a few grindings of nutmeg.

Pour the mixture into serving bowls. Heat the rest of the butter in a small pan and fry the sage leaves until crisp. Spoon the butter and the leaves over the top of the pâté and place in the fridge overnight.

White Bean and Tuna Salad
(I like to use white tuna in olive oil but ordinary tuna in spring water or olive oil is fine, but not brine. Again, you can make this the day before and store in the fridge.)

400g (14oz) dried cannellini beans; 2 onions, quartered;
3 bay leaves; 1 tbsp fresh thyme; 500g (1lb 2oz) tinned tuna,

drained; 2 large red onions, thinly sliced into rings; a handful of chopped flat leaf parsley; 4 tbsp capers; freshly ground
salt and pepper.

Dressing: 3 cloves garlic, crushed and finely chopped; juice
of 2 lemons; 150ml (5fl oz) olive oil; freshly ground salt
and pepper.

You could buy tins of ready-to-use beans but it's so easy
to prepare the dried ones and the flavour is infinitely
better. Soak them overnight in plenty of cold water. The
next morning drain and place in saucepan with the quartered onions, bay leaves and thyme (don't add any salt, it
toughens the skin), bring to the boil and simmer for about
an hour and a half under they are tender. Soak the capers
in milk to remove the brine.

Whilst the beans are cooking, make the dressing. Put
all the ingredients in a blender and whizz until thoroughly combined. When the beans are tender drain them thoroughly, remove the onions, thyme and bay leaves and tip
them into a large bowl. Pour the dressing over the beans
whilst still warm (so they soak up all the flavours).

Drain the tuna and flake it into largish chunks. If you
are making this the day before stop now and place everything in the fridge. To finish, combine the beans, onion
rings and the parsley. Check the seasoning and serve in a
large bowl with a few capers sprinkled over the top.

Mozzarella and Tomato Salad with Pesto

8 mozzarella di bufala, or regular mozzarella but please, not the Danish stuff; 6 large, ripe beef tomatoes; 100g (4oz) fresh basil leaves; 1 large clove of garlic, crushed; 2 tbsp pine kernels; 150ml (5fl oz) extra virgin olive oil; 50g (2oz) grated Parmesan.

Place most of the basil leaves (reserving some for the garnish), the garlic, pine kernels and olive oil in a blender with a grind or two of sea salt and blend until smooth. Pour into a bowl and stir in the Parmesan. Slice the mozzarella and the beef tomatoes into rounds and arrange on a platter in a circular pattern, alternating one with the other until it covers the whole plate. (You will probably need more than one.) Finish off with finely shredded basil leaves scattered over the top and a drizzle of pesto.

Gammon in Cider with a Mustard and Caramelised Apple Crust

I love the combination of pork with apples and a natural progression of that is gammon cooked in cider. The end result is both sweet and moist. (This can be made up to 3 days before the party.)

4kg (9lb) mild-cure gammon (take it out of the fridge at least 3 hours before cooking); 4 litres (7 pints) sweet cider, reserve 4 tbsp; 2 onions, peeled and cut in half; 2 bay leaves; 150g

(5oz) fresh breadcrumbs; 200g (7oz) dark muscovado sugar; 2 tbsp mustard powder; 4 tbsp Dijon mustard; 2 large Bramley cooking apples.

You will need a big, big pot for this, if you don't own one then beg, steal or borrow one from friends or family. Mild-cure gammon doesn't need soaking, which is always a bonus as I hate doing that kind of stuff. Put the gammon in the pan skin-side down, add the onion halves and the bay leaves, pour over the cider, bring to the boil then simmer with the lid, on but slightly askew, for about 3½ hours.

Preheat the oven to 180°C (350°F). When the ham is done take it out of the pot, let it cool, then remove the skin leaving just a very thin layer of white fat. Mix the breadcrumbs, sugar and mustards to a thick paste and add the reserved cider drop by drop (you don't want a runny mixture but a stiff paste). Spread the paste over the top of the ham. Peel and core the apples, slice thinly into half-moon shapes and place in overlapping rows over the crust. Place on a roasting tray and cook in a hot oven for 20 minutes.

Lemon Roasted Chicken with Garlic and Rosemary
This couldn't be easier and the smell that permeates the house whilst it cooks will have everyone drooling.

50 chicken portions (drumsticks and thighs are best, bone in). Marinade: 6 garlic cloves, crushed and finely chopped;

200ml (7fl oz) olive oil; 100ml (3½fl oz) lemon juice; 1 hand-ful rosemary leaves, finely chopped; freshly ground salt and pepper.

The day before the party, combine all the ingredients for the marinade, mixing well. Slash the skin on the chicken portions using a sharp knife and coat with the marinade, use your hands to ensure the chicken is well coated. Cover with cling film and leave in the fridge for 24 hours.

About 2 hours before the party heat the oven to 180°C (350°F) and cook the chicken for 30 to 40 minutes until the juices run clear and the skin is crispy. Keep in a warm place until you serve.

Smoked Salmon Ceviche with Wasabi, Honey and Lime

A friend recently served this at a New Year's party and it made a refreshing change to plain smoked salmon. Wasabi is Japanese horseradish and is normally eaten alongside sushi and sashimi; it's brain-numbingly fiery, so use spar-ingly. It is now available in most supermarkets.

A whole side of smoked salmon (if you can carve, so much the better, otherwise buy it pre-sliced); 50ml (2fl oz) lime juice; 25ml (1fl oz) soy sauce; 3 tbsp good-quality runny honey; Wasabi; an iceberg lettuce taken apart leaf by leaf.

Whisk together the soy sauce, lime juice and honey. Add the Wasabi little by little and taste it, it should be evident but not so much that your head explodes.

Arrange the smoked salmon on platters and drizzle with the marinade – not too much, don't drown it. Leave it in the fridge, basting from time to time until the lime has 'cooked' the salmon and it becomes opaque. Arrange on a serving platter atop whole iceberg lettuce leaves. Serve with lime wedges garnished with watercress.

Oven-baked Mediterranean Vegetables with Balsamic and Muscovado Sugar

This tastes far better if made the day before, giving the flavours time to infuse.

4 large aubergines, cut into 2in dice; 6 courgettes cut into 1in rounds; 20 shallots, unpeeled; 4 sweet potatoes cut into 2in dice; 2 of red, yellow and green peppers cut into large 2in squares; 20 whole garlic cloves, unpeeled.

Marinade: 300ml (10fl oz) balsamic vinegar; 100g (4oz) muscovado sugar; 200ml (7fl oz) olive oil; 3 cloves garlic, crushed; a handful of fresh rosemary, finely chopped; 2 tbsp chopped fresh sage; 2 tbsp chopped fresh thyme; freshly ground salt and pepper.

145

Heat the oven to 170°C (325°F). Once you have chopped all your veggies place them in a large bowl (probably a clean, unused washing-up bowl given the quantities). Leave the shallots and garlic unpeeled as when cooked whole they become incredibly sweet and ooze out of their skins. Combine all the ingredients for the marinade and pour over the chopped veggies, making sure they are all well covered. Place the veggies in large oven trays and bake in a medium oven for 30 minutes until the vegetables are tender, but not too soft. When cooked and cooled place them once again in the washing-up bowl, this time line it with tin foil and keep in a cool place.

New Potato and Spring Onion Salad
The potatoes can be cooked the day before, but don't dress them until the afternoon of the party or you'll end up with a soggy mess.

4kg (9lb) of small new potatoes; 20 spring onions, very finely chopped; 6 tbsp finely chopped parsley; 6 tbsp finely chopped chives.

Dressing: 300ml (10fl oz) olive oil; 100ml (3½fl oz) white wine vinegar; 3 tbsp Dijon mustard; freshly ground salt and black pepper to taste.

Wash the potatoes well, but don't peel or scrape them. Place in large saucepan with salt and pour boiling water over them until it reaches about halfway up the pan. Cover and allow to simmer for around 25 minutes until tender.

Whilst the potatoes are cooking prepare the dressing, combine all the ingredients and whisk. When the potatoes are cooked drain them well and place in a shallow tray, dressing them whilst still warm so they absorb all the flavours. Check the seasoning and allow to cool, mixing in the parsley and spring onion just before serving.

Mixed Leaf Salad

Try and use as many different kinds of leaves as possible, a good selection would be at least five of the following: cos lettuce, rocket, gem lettuce, mizuna, lollo rosso, chicory, watercress, dandelion leaves or anything else you can find. There are no hard and fast rules, just make it colourful and interesting. Allow a handful per person.

Wash and dry the leaves thoroughly, place in a large salad bowl and mix them up. Don't dress the salad as it will go soggy in no time; instead, place a jug of dressing by the side of the bowl and let people help themselves.

It's hard to give quantities for a dressing as it depends on the volume of salad, but the rule of thumb is always one third vinegar to olive oil. Use balsamic, white or red wine vinegar and the best extra virgin olive oil you can find – I always add a level teaspoon of sugar, it's a family thing.

Rub the salad bowl with a clove of garlic rather than

putting it in the dressing, it's too strong raw. Don't forget a
good grinding of rock salt and freshly ground black pepper.

HOT

Penne con Salsicce al Forno (Oven-baked penne with sausage)

A simple rustic dish using spicy Italian sausages that can
be prepared up to 2 or 3 days in advance.

2kg (4lb) penne, cooked.

Sausage ragu: 8 onions, finely chopped; 6 cloves garlic,
finely chopped; 4 celery stalks, finely chopped; 2 tbsp thyme,
finely chopped; 1 tbsp dried oregano; 1kg (2lb 4oz) Italian
sausages, cut into 1in slices, skinned; 4 x 400g (14oz) tinned
tomatoes, sieved; 50ml (2fl oz) olive oil.

Béchamel: 2 litres (3½ pints) milk; 2 carrots; 1 large onion,
halved; 1 stick of celery; 15 whole black peppercorns; 3 bay
leaves; 200g (7oz) butter; nutmeg; freshly ground salt and
pepper; 3 mozzarella cheeses; 60g (2oz) grated fresh
Parmesan.

Sausage Ragu: in a large, heavy-bottomed saucepan heat
the oil and gently fry the onion, garlic and celery over a

low heat until soft. In a separate pan brown the sausages before setting them aside on kitchen paper. Drain the residual oil from the frying pan and deglaze with a large glass of red wine, allowing it to bubble and reduce by half. Once the onion is soft, add the herbs, sieved tomatoes, red wine juices and the sausages, stir well and bring to the boil. Allow to simmer very gently for 2 hours. If it gets a little dry add some hot stock made with one Kallo stock cube.

Béchemel: place the milk, onion, celery, bay leaves and peppercorns into a saucepan and bring to the boil very slowly. When boiled set aside for an hour and allow to infuse. Strain into a clean pan and keep warm over a low heat.

Melt the butter over a medium heat and stir in the flour off the heat with a wooden spoon so it forms a glossy paste, place back on the heat and whisk in the warm milk a little at a time until it has all been incorporated and the sauce is smooth. Season with freshly ground salt, pepper and a few generous gratings of nutmeg.

When the sausage ragu is cooked combine a generous half of it with the cooked penne, mixing well, then divide the pasta amongst 2 or 3 large ovenproof dishes. Place a thick layer of ragu on top of the pasta, ensuring it is evenly divided between all the dishes. Top this with evenly scattered circles of thinly sliced mozzarella and then spread béchamel sauce over the whole thing. Finally, add a dusting of grated Parmesan.

I suggest you make these two days before the party and store in the fridge. Take them out about 2 hours before you need them to get them to room temperature and cook in a hot oven for about an hour, or until the whole thing pulsates and bubbles and the top is golden brown.

DESSERT BUFFET

Paola's Chocolate Pudding

Fresh Fruit Kebabs

Pavlova

CHEESEBOARD

*Stilton, Mature Cheddar, Dolcelatte, Brie,
Chèvre, Taleggio*

Paola's Chocolate Pudding

I don't have a sweet tooth, my sister is the patissier in our family. This is one of her favourite recipes, and one of the few desserts I can't resist. It couldn't be easier to make and it tastes like heaven.

600g (1lb 4oz) 70 per cent cocoa solids, dark chocolate; 8 tsp instant coffee; 4 tbsp boiling water; 200g (7oz) caster sugar; 200g (7oz) unsalted butter; 8 eggs; 100ml (4fl oz) brandy/Marsala/rum (any of them will do) mixed with 100ml (4fl oz) water; Petit Beurre biscuits.

Melt the chocolate in a glass bowl over a pan of simmering water, dissolve the coffee in the boiling water and add to the chocolate. Whisk in the sugar, butter and eggs and beat until well mixed. Lightly soak the biscuits in the brandy and water, but not too much, they shouldn't be too soggy.

Line 4 loaf tins with cling film (although if you have a pan big enough you could just make one large one). Pour in a layer of the chocolate mixture, follow with a layer of biscuits and repeat until the tin is full. Refrigerate overnight. To turn out, lift the cling film out and peel away, it should be a perfectly packed, rectangular slice of chocolate heaven.

Fresh Fruit Kebabs
Wonderfully refreshing and colourful, these kebabs look fabulous on the table and any leftovers can easily be transformed into smoothies the next morning to ease any hangovers.

Strawberries, kiwi, pineapple, grapes, mint leaves, 8in wooden skewers.

Intersperse the fruit on the skewers with mint leaves and arrange on a platter. For a party of 50 I would make around 30 kebabs. If the strawberries are large, cut them in half.

I once saw these served at a lunch buffet at the Grand Hyatt, Singapore and next to the kebabs sat a chocolate fountain which is exactly that; a fountain of cascading molten chocolate to dip the kebabs in. You could melt some chocolate, whisk in a little butter and double cream and leave it in a bowl for people to dunk their fruit kebabs in.

Pavlova

Pavlova always looks great and is relatively easy to make. For really good results make sure your egg whites are as fresh as possible.

> 6 egg whites; 350g (12oz) caster sugar; 600ml (1 pint) double cream, whipped; 800g (1lb 8oz) mix of strawberries, raspberries and blackberries; 1 passion fruit.

Preheat the oven to 150°C (300°F). Lightly oil 2 baking trays and line with baking paper or silicone paper. Place the egg whites in a bowl and whisk until they form soft peaks and you can upturn the bowl without them falling out. Add the sugar one tablespoon at a time, whisking after each one until it is all incorporated. Spoon the meringue mixture onto the prepared baking sheets, drawing circles of about 20cm in diameter. Spoon blobs of meringue around the outside so that they join up to form a circle. Make swirly peaks over the top of the cake using a fork. Place the meringues in the oven and cook for an hour then turn off the oven and leave them in there to cool until totally cold, preferably overnight.

To assemble the pavlovas, lift the meringues from the baking sheet and place on serving dishes. Just before serving, spread whipped cream over the top and scatter with the soft fruit. Spoon out the pulp from the passion fruit and sprinkle artistically over the whole thing.

Cheeseboard

Choose your own selection of cheeses, just make sure they vary in texture, colour and shape – although I do recommend sticking with a whole Brie as it just looks so fabulous on the table. Take the cheese out of the fridge in the afternoon and leave it outside, covered: cheese can get very smelly in a hot kitchen.

Serve it on a large wooden board with grapes, pears, apples, celery, dried figs and apricots and, of course, Carr's water biscuits and some digestives. I have a total aversion to those big tins of cheese biscuits they are too naff to ever be retro. But it's up to you, I can see their value in a party situation, though while you're at it you may as well serve cheese and pineapple on sticks . . .

PET NAMES

☙

Cootchy, Cootchy Coo . . .

A rose by any other name would smell as sweet.
WILLIAM SHAKESPEARE

The Middle is the time that those inevitable 'pet names' you call each other really come into their own (come on, admit it, you've done it). I wonder if we would 'do' the pet name thing if we realised just how dumb we sounded. It's sad when we get so used to calling someone Snookums that, sod decorum or propriety, we use it all the time, especially when we really shouldn't. Snookums is ok in the privacy of one's own home, but it has absolutely no place in public.

I should quit whilst I am ahead, but I simply can't. Therefore, for your delight and delectation below please find some of the more inventive pet names with which my exes have saddled me. (You know who you are.)

Sancia Pancia	(Roughly translated it means big belly. Charming.)
Smelly Bum	(This man was in love with me?)
Little Lix	(Cute until I realised 'Lix' was being used as a verb.)
Hot Shot	(Well, I am hot.)
Barry	(I have no idea and don't ever wish to know.)
Contessa	(The man had style.)
Schrumple	(Weirdo.)
Riviera Girl	(You gotta love that!)
Tartlet	(I object!)

FOREVER FRIENDS

All For One and One For All

My true friends have always given me that supreme
proof of devotion – a spontaneous aversion
to the man I love.

COLETTE

Ah yes, where would we be without our friends? That close-knit circle of confidantes who love us unconditionally, come rain or shine, the chosen few who have stuck by us through thick and thin, who know us inside out and have been there for us at the beginning and, sadly, the demise, of every single relationship we have ever had. Who, in fact, have witnessed in full Technicolor the good, the bad and the end!

And, I'm afraid, therein lies the rub.

When we decide to take yet another chance on love and introduce our *new* partner to our *old* friends, to those people who have been party to every loved-up stupor we've ever been in, there is a chance they might be just a little bit sceptical; their faith in our new-found happiness just a teensy-weensy bit jaundiced until they get to know him a little better.

No matter how sure *you* are that this time it's for real, your friends probably won't be totally convinced at the outset. In fact, they will almost certainly be busy looking out for your best interests rather than viewing your new relationship objectively, in the vain hope of protecting from you from the possibility of yet another broken heart.

Save, save, oh save me from the Candid Friend.

Geoorge Canning

The ensuing conversation tends to be quite one-sided and goes something like this;

'*This time it's different, this time it feels so right. He's kind, gorgeous, sexy and he makes me laugh.*'

'*We just have this incredibly deep connection.*'

'*I did not say that last time.*'

'*Did I?*'

'*Well, this time I really mean it.*'

I rest my case.

Our friends don't really stand a chance: we want them to like him as much as we do and we don't really want to hear it if they don't.

The problem is that throughout Pink Cloud we are so wrapped up in each other that we hardly see our friends at all, and when we do our conversation revolves around our new love affair and how *fabulous* life is, how *fabulous* he is, how *fabulous* the sex is, in fact, how *bloody fabulous* everything is. Don't feel bad, everyone in Pink Cloud acts the same way and, yes, it's bloody irritating but somehow we all manage to put up with each other.

The proper office of a friend is to side with you
when you are wrong.
Nearly everybody will side with you when you are right.

OSCAR WILDE

The upshot of all this is that your mates could be a tad peeved at your reclusiveness over the past few months, after all, how can they tell whether they like him or not if they haven't had the chance to get to know him.

It's time everyone got together and had some fun. I suggest you host a Games Night, which is akin to a children's birthday party, but with booze and much better food.

Invite your closest friends, organise some really silly games, cook a casual dinner, get everyone to bring some wine and you have the makings of a fun and highly enter-taining getting-to-know-ya kind of evening. Playing games breaks the ice and is good bonding material. (No, not bondage, that's something else entirely and for another book!)

So you've got good food, good wine, good friends and some riotous games to play. Your friends are going to love him.

Don't forget; playing childhood games can still be a lot of fun when you are older.

Musical Chairs: Use plastic garden chairs, I found to my cost that wooden dining chairs resemble firewood after a particu-larly fierce bout of this, given that adult bottoms are so much larger and heavier.

Pass the Parcel: The adult version can be a lot of fun if you're just a little cheeky and a touch suggestive with the hidden pressies. I suggest a trip to Ann Summers.

Blind Man's Buff: There's a blindfold involved and bunch of adults who've probably had a little too much to drink, it can't fail to be a hoot.

Hide 'n' Seek: A good opportunity to find a quiet corner and not get found!

Pass the Orange under the Chin: Ok, I have never really under-stood the logic behind this game either, but every time I have been forced into playing it has never failed to end up with hysterical laughter, much banter and a really good vibe.

Spin the Bottle: As the night wears on there's nothing like a good game of Spin the Bottle, now there's an icebreaker. Make sure you have a truly filthy cocktail should the player choose a forfeit rather than a kiss. Chicken!

I'm aware that the above all sounds very, very silly indeed, but I promise that if you take a group of people who don't know each other and want them to end up as bosom buddies, a Games Night is the way forward.

Food-wise, I always make the same thing (it's now a bit of a tradition), a huge pot of Chilli con Carne with all the trimmings. It can be made days in advance and left to its own devices on the hob until you are ready to eat. I prefer to serve it buffet-style and let everyone help themselves.

Chilli con Carne

I love a good chilli but I get so disappointed when people don't serve it in the same way that I do. That makes me sound somewhat truculent but I do think that the accompaniments are just as important, if not more important, than the actual chilli itself.

It's hard to be exact about the quantity of chillies you need to use to get the desired heat as they can vary quite dramatically. Use your own judgement, the finished dish needs to be hot, but not inedible.

I once went to a party where chilli was the main course but it was prepared by a man with an asbestos palate. It was so hot that no one could eat it, which was rather a shame as he had made enough to feed the 5,000. I do hope he didn't end up giving it to the dog!

The large red chillies are generally quite mild, but taste them as you're chopping in case you get a rogue one. The little red bird's eye chillies, on the other hand, are very hot indeed so if you prefer a milder flavour only use half of one and add more halfway through cooking if needed. Chocolate may sound like a strange addition but it works really well, adding another subtle layer of flavour that is authentically Mexican. The quantities in this recipe should feed 12 people.

1.5kg (3lb) braising or chuck steak, finely chopped but not minced; 650g (1½lb) dried red kidney beans; 4 large Spanish onions, finely chopped; 4 large red chillies, deseeded and finely chopped; 2 large red peppers, deseeded and finely chopped; 1 bird's eye red chilli, deseeded and finely chopped; 3 tsp paprika; 5 cloves garlic, crushed and finely chopped; 2 x 400g (14oz) tinned tomatoes; 6 squares 70 per cent cocoa solids dark chocolate; 150ml (5fl oz) tomato purée; 1.5 litres (2½ pints) chicken stock, either fresh or made with Kallo stock cubes; 50ml (2fl oz) olive oil; salt and freshly ground pepper.

Heat the oven to 160°C (325°F). Cover the beans with cold water and bring to the boil. Simmer for 15 minutes, turn off the heat and allow them to soak for an hour, then drain.

In a heavy-bottomed saucepan heat the oil and gently cook the onions and garlic until soft, then combine with the chillies and peppers. Turn up the heat a little and brown the meat, then add the chopped tomatoes, tomato purée, stock, paprika, broken-up chocolate, beans, salt and freshly ground pepper. Give it a good stir, bring it to a gentle simmer and transfer to the oven for approximately 3 hours, checking it once an hour or so. If it's a little dry, add a small amount of stock or boiling water.

And now for the side dishes. These are my own creation, I just can't enjoy a chilli without them.

Spicy Potato Wedges

3kg (6½lb) floury potatoes, washed, scrubbed and cut into wedges; 4 tsp paprika; 2 tsp cayenne pepper; 2 tsp ground cumin; 2 cloves garlic, crushed and finely chopped; 2 large mild red chillies, deseeded and cut into fine strips; 100ml (4fl oz) olive oil; salt and freshly ground pepper.

Preheat the oven to 200°C (400°F) and place the potato wedges in a roasting tin. Combine all the other ingredients and pour over the potatoes, coating them thoroughly. Place in the oven and cook for 35–40 minutes until crispy and golden on the outside and soft in the middle. Scatter with the sliced red chilli, season with salt and freshly ground black pepper and serve in a large brightly-coloured bowl.

You will also need:

A bowl of sour cream
A bowl of grated mature cheddar
Garlic bread
Tortilla chips

I know these accompaniments are not very authentic and I'm sure many of you would prefer rice and peas, that's fine too.

Jelly and Ice-cream

No, I'm not joking, nothing goes down quite as well as jelly and ice-cream at a kids' party or, for that matter, at an adults' one.

I could give you a terribly complicated recipe for a posh jelly made with leaf gelatine and champagne, but I'm not going to because what we want at a Games Night is the real thing; jewel-coloured jellies made from those rubber-like cubes that you buy in squares and dissolve in boiling water. But I would suggest you make your jelly a little more interesting by adding fresh fruit to the mix: strawberries, raspberries or pineapple (but if you use pineapple make sure it's tinned and use the juice as part of the liquid for making up the jelly), or perhaps you could spice it up with some fresh chilli or other unusual flavourings. Be imaginative.

I like to make individual jellies just like we had as kids, rather than one big one, and I always make a batch or two with vodka instead of water. I recommend using half the amount of liquid to yield a really firm jelly with a huge kick which can be used as prizes or forfeits during the games.

N.B. Dissolve the jelly cubes in a little boiling water before adding the vodka at room temperature.

An alternative, equally risible but truly historic, dessert is that Seventies classic, Angel Delight. I recently resurrected it at a *Sex and the City* night I held; which involved a group of very tipsy girlies watching hours and hours of the now defunct show on DVD. (I still can't believe it's over.) Everyone loved it. Butterscotch is still by far the best flavour, quickly followed by strawberry.

DOMESTIC BLISS?

⟡

Domestic Minefield

*A guy gets married and the morning after his
wedding night, goes into the bathroom and finds
a dead horse in the bathtub. He runs out says,
'Darling there's a dead horse in the bathtub.'
And his wife replies, 'Well, I never said
I was neat.'*

WALTER MATTHAU

The realities of living together generally hit home
after the first few months, when the novelty factor
starts to wear off and we become aware of what it really
means to share our living space and the minutiae of our
lives with another human being.

As I said earlier, life would be pretty boring if we were

all the same and did things in the same way. Thankfully, we are all one of a kind and our differing lifestyles are a reflection of our individuality. We have our own habits and our unique day-to-day routines; this is not a bad thing, but it does mean that some concessions need to be made when two people who are used to living alone decide to set up shop together.

We have already discussed some of the positive aspects of living together: the feelings of security and stability, moving into a lovely new home, never being lonely, having someone to lean on when we need support and someone to blow our noses when we are poorly; it's all just peachy.

Except those few occasions when it isn't.

When we share a home with another person, male or female, we have to adjust a little to their habits, just as they have to adjust to ours. The period of transition as we find out exactly what those habits are can, on occasion, be a tad trying for both parties.

There are certain patterns of behaviour, little things I grant you but, nonetheless, things which when repeated daily and compounded by lots of other little things, can get on our very last nerve and lead to the mother of all showdowns.

The niggly things that drive us crazy are generally pretty petty. Things like, squeezing the toothpaste from the top, leaving a trail of toast crumbs in the butter, putting empty milk cartons back in the fridge, *every time*! Him leaving the loo seat up *again*, her blunting his new 3-blade razor when shaving her legs, his continually-growing mountain of paper, her pathological need for uncluttered surfaces, his socks strewn over the floor, the plughole in the shower constantly blocked by her long hair and the Sunday papers ending up like confetti after being read by one but, unfortunately, not yet by the other.

Petty? Perhaps. Irritating? Beyond belief.

Then, of course, there's *that* issue, probably one of the biggest bugbears for all newly cohabiting couples. Yes, that's right, I'm talking about the dreaded, mind-numbing misery that is housework.

Unless you can afford a cleaner, which, frankly, if you're both working I suggest you probably *can* and definitely should *do* forthwith. Domestic harmony can be a domestic minefield.

Don't cook. Don't clean. No man will ever make love to a woman because she's waxed the linoleum. 'My God that floor is immaculate. Lie down you hot bitch.'

JOAN RIVERS

I refuse to countenance the old adage that women are more houseproud or more accomplished at performing household tasks than men. That's a load of codswallop.

Men are just as capable of hoovering, dusting, washing-up or ironing as a human being with breasts, namely, a woman. You don't need ovaries to wash-up.

Of course, there are some really slatternly women around, women for whom the very idea of housework is a total anathema. Conversely, there are men who are tidy to the point of being neurotic and others who live like pigs and, of course, we all of us know women who are so extreme in their quest for cleanliness that they cling film the loo once they've cleaned it in a bid to keep it sterile.

It takes all kinds.

The problem occurs when one person's idea of a clean house is someone else's idea of a health hazard.

I, for example, like my home to be relatively tidy but also comfortably lived in. I clean up as I go along but I don't hyperventilate if I haven't hoovered for three or four days. I once had a fridge magnet that said, 'Dull women have immaculate houses.' Hear, hear!

My personal bête noir is ironing. I hate it, I would rather chew off my left foot than waste valuable living time ironing; I'm very much the iron-it-as-I-need-it type. I marvel at my sister, who even irons tea towels and knickers – for the love of God, why?

My other household tragedy is my wardrobe. I have no idea why it is always unfailingly chaotic; my theory is that my clothes are secretly breeding behind my back.

DOMESTIC BLISS?

*I hate housework. You make the beds, you do the dishes
and six months later you have to start all over again.*

JOAN RIVERS

Ok, so all in all I don't think I'm too hard to live with, not
perfect, but neither too slovenly nor too fixated in the
housework department, but I hate, detest and abhor
clutter. I just can't relax in a house that is awash with bits
of paper, magazines, old bills, letters, 3-month-old newspapers and a collection of knick-knacks that pass as ornaments, but in reality are nothing more than a bunch of
dust collectors and generally in very poor taste.
Ornaments are the bane of my life; what is the point of
them? What purpose do they serve?

The way I live isn't necessarily *right*, but it is right for
me and I really can't imagine changing. It would seem that
the older we get and the longer we live alone, the harder
it is to compromise.

So what would happen if I fell in love and set up home
with a wonderful man whose idea of housework involves
a quick flick of the duster once a month, hoovering only
when the plain carpet starts to look patterned, and who
likes to keep every last ticket stub, newsletter, pizza menu,
work papers, newspapers and indeed any bloody papers
strewn all over the house because, well that's just how he
likes to live and my obsession with clutter-free surfaces is
making him crazy?

I'm almost ashamed to admit this, but no matter how much I loved him I would have to kill him if he didn't see the error of his ways and ensure that the paper mountain was transformed into a very small, perfectly-formed hill. Pronto!

Conversely, if his life was to be spared I would have to tidy up around him, which would drive us both nuts and the resentment factor on both sides would build and build until it blew, not unlike like Krakatoa on a bad day.

To be frank, there is no easy solution to this domestic dilemma as we both have as much right to live under our joint roof in the manner in which we see fit and to which we have become accustomed.

So, here it is folks, here's the compromise.

A propos the clutter and bits of paper we could allocate one room exclusively for him where he can build the paper mountain he so clearly needs to construct. A room where he can be as messy as he wants, a room, therefore, that I simply do not enter on the understanding that the other rooms in the house remain relatively clutter-free.

I will also put up with a few well-placed, though frankly pointless, ornaments if it keeps him happy and I promise not to accidentally-on-purpose break any of them. That would be so childish, wouldn't it?

The most popular labour-saving device
today is still money.

JOEY ADAMS

So now I'm going to share with you the three golden rules that will guarantee domestic harmony in any home and will ensure that you never have to have a discussion about whose turn it is to clean the loo.

1. Get a cleaner.
2. Get a cleaner.
3. Get a cleaner

SOUL MATES

Together 4 Ever

> *You complete me.*
> JERRY MAGUIRE

Some people are made for each other, you can tell just by looking at them that they are soul mates. After a while these couples even start to look alike and can finish off each other's sentences, almost reading each other's minds.

The same could be said for certain foods whose combination is so divine they must surely be culinary soul mates. These are some of my personal favourites, some of which are perhaps more obvious than others but I urge you to try them all. (A few of these are a ménage à trois – nothing wrong with a little experimenting now and again.)

Poached eggs and steamed asparagus
Jellied eels, fresh chilli and lemon juice
Hot Ribena and dark rum
Smoked salmon and horseradish
Roast chicken and lemon
Chicken broth and grated Parmesan
Roasted onions and balsamic vinegar
Fillet steak and watercress
Cold roast lamb and Dijon mustard
Dried fruit and cinnamon
Hot milk and honey
Buttered toast and lemon and sugar
Coconut cream, coriander and chilli
Oysters and Tabasco
Strawberries and champagne
Stilton and celery
Fresh mango and lime juice
Roasted vegetables and honey
Risotto and dried porcini mushrooms
Mashed potato and nutmeg
Fish fingers and peas
Baked figs and prosciutto
Prawns and garlic butter
Panettone and white wine
Roast turkey, coleslaw and mango chutney
Fresh foie gras and apples
Bananas and custard

Cheese and pears
Pumpkin and cardamom
Mussels and chips
Boiled eggs and anchovies
A sandwich of toasted cheese, bacon and strawberry jam
Hot chocolate with instant coffee

EATING AL FRESCO

❦

Perfect Picnics

There is not enough time to do all of the nothing that we want to do.

BILL WATTERSON

There is something magical about waking up on a summer morning with the one you love and deciding, to hell with it, sod the shopping/decorating/ cleaning or whatever other boring task we *should* be doing on this glorious Saturday morning, household chores be damned: we're going on a picnic, just the two of us.

There may well be nothing in the fridge but as my picnics tend to come straight out of the local deli, that's not a problem. Television chefs are always banging on about menus for picnics which is fine except that, as with most things in my life, picnics are very much spur of the moment affairs that leave me very little time to prepare. I'm sure this is the case with most people, although having said that I can't be doing with a picnic that consists of shop-bought sandwiches, a packet of crisps, a Mars Bar and a diet coke. That's not a picnic, that's a packed lunch, which is not the same thing at all.

As I said, my idea of a picnic is to wander into my local deli and buy a ready-cooked roast chicken, a few slices of ham carved off the bone, some smoked salmon and add to it a couple of boiled eggs. (A picnic just doesn't feel like a picnic without boiled eggs.) I also pack some very ripe vine tomatoes, a pot of coleslaw, a good mix of salad leaves packed into a Tupperware container (am I the only person in the world who feels like a 'proper' little house-wife when I use Tupperware?), and a carefully washed out, empty medicine bottle filled with balsamic vinegar and olive oil.

In terms of condiments I like some mango chutney and English mustard for the chicken and ham respectively, some lemon wedges and horseradish for the smoked salmon, some salt and pepper and, of course, some really good bread, perhaps two or three different types. I always take two bottles of chilled wine and at least two bottles of frozen water. I keep bottles of Evian in the freezer all through the summer as I like it icy cold and on a picnic they not only keep everything else cold, but they ensure that you have chilled water all day long. You also need strawberries and some kind of cake for tea. Put everything in an insulated picnic bag or coolbox; pretty wicker hampers are all very well but they don't keep anything chilled and are unpractical as they are generally too small.

I can happily spend endless summer days stretched out in the sun with a picnic by my side. (Although this may be somewhat surprising to people who have been on a picnic with me and witnessed my pathological fear of creepy crawlies and the fact that I have been known to sit in the car with all the windows shut until the killer bee that is quite happily minding his own business, buzzing around at least 10 yards from me, has taken his leave.) But, despite the wildlife, I am never happier than when I am packing up a cold box on a gorgeous summer's day so that me and mine can eat and drink al fresco, literally until the cows come home.

I would love to be able to describe to you the secluded country meadows I seek out in a bid to escape the rat race that is London, but, being a city girl through and through, most of my idyllic picnics take place at the epicentre of Boho-Cool that is Primrose Hill. Despite being located exactly 10 minutes from my home, once I'm lying on that grassy knoll basking in the sunshine, glass in hand and whispering sweet nothings to the one I love I could be any-where in the world except, of course, when I take in the spectacular views across what could only be London town.

One of the things I love most about picnics 'on the hill' is the high-octane people-watching factor, especially on Saturday afternoons. The beautiful people start to arrive at around 4pm (not for them the glare and harmful rays of the midday sun), they are, of course, immaculately turned out, with their tousled blonde hair, perfect teeth and blindingly white t-shirts worn with teeny tiny shorts – and that's just the boys.

These elegant and flawless beings tend to move in packs and by early evening there are large groups of them scattered all over the hill; chatting, drinking, prancing, preening and generally putting on a bit of a show for the mere mortals that have been there since 10am, are now burnt to a crisp and more than a tad tipsy. (There are 4 off-licences in walking distance.)

Then, like clockwork, at 6 o'clock the smell of charred wood fills the air as barbecues are lit and the cognoscenti set about the task of cooking themselves dinner. They favour those little foil trays filled with charcoal that you can buy at petrol stations and most supermarkets. On the surface these look rubbish but in fact they do quite a good job, especially if you've two of them going at the same time and you add some smoked hickory briquettes or handfuls of dried rosemary to the coals. All manner of food is prepared on the hill and the maddeningly aromatic scent of barbecues is nearly as gorgeous as the people doing the cooking.

I tend to be one of the get-there-by-10, tipsy-by-5 crowd but recently I partook in the late afternoon barbecue of some very trendy Boho friends. Sitting there at dusk, watching the sun set over London whilst nibbling on a perfectly-cooked sausage wasn't half bad and it was actually very romantic, especially as I caught sight of Jude and Sienna strolling up the hill hand-in-hand. If it's good enough for Jude, it's good enough for me.

Swoon.

So, here are some ideas for a stylish, Boho barbecue worthy of the beautiful people.

I like to stick with the tried and tested barbecue formula that is sausages, chicken and burgers as it's easy to pack and transport and quick to cook, but honey, forget the Joneses, if you want to keep up with the Judes and Siennas you can't serve just any old sausage.

Firstly, it has to be organic, don't even think about trying to get away with an own-brand, supermarket pork banger. To get it right you need to avail yourself of some spicy Italian sausages from an obscure part of Tuscany or, better yet, Umbria, or some handmade venison sausages from a butcher you know by name that fills its own skins and can tell you where each animal was born and what star sign they were. At a push you can just about get away with those organic snags that carry the appellation and royal stamp of our future king. The humble banger has gone upmarket and jolly good they are too.

N.B. No matter what the occasion you should never, under any circumstances, buy sausages with a meat content of less than 80 per cent. They tend to be a little more expensive but they're worth it to avoid the crap that goes into bangers with a lesser meat content.

If you're serving burgers, make them yourself using ground rump steak. Add some sautéed onions to the raw meat plus seasoning, shape into rounds and stick them in the fridge for an hour or so to set. I use ciabatta to accommodate my burgers, get one of those parcooked loaves from any supermarket, split it in half and toast the cut side on the barbecue until just golden. In the true manner of Boho-chic add some thinly sliced goat's cheese and a handful of rocket leaves to the finished burger and, to hell with being cool, I can't resist a dollop of ketchup and one of mayo.

I recommend boned thighs if you are cooking chicken, which are both flavoursome and quick to cook.

Whisk up a marinade combining 300ml (10fl oz) orange juice; 2 tbsp tomato purée; 2 cloves garlic, finely chopped; 50ml (2fl oz) sweet chilli sauce; 1in finely chopped ginger; 25ml (1oz) soy sauce; 1 crumbled Kallo chicken stock cube; runny honey; salt and freshly ground pepper. If you like it hot, add a finely sliced fresh red chilli.

Slash the chicken skin in several places and rub the marinade into it. Cover with cling film, set aside and allow the flavours to infuse.

The vegetarians amongst us who eschew such a meat-fest needn't feel left out, the barbecue is also great for cooking haloumi, corn on the cob wrapped in tin foil, veggie kebabs or even large portobello mushrooms with some garlic butter.

To accompany this barbecued food, pack up some unusual salad leaves (dandelion, mizuna and radicchio are currently very bling), some Polaine (a sourdough bread which is terribly trendy and also really good), some tinnies of Nastro Azzuro Italian beer, a couple of bottles of Cloudy Bay Sauvignon Blanc from Marlborough, New Zealand, and some San Pellegrino sparkling water.

Baby, you've arrived and you're so Boho it hurts.

I couldn't possibly discuss picnics without giving you my mother's famous and utterly delicious Torta di Patate (Potato Cake).

Throughout my childhood my family were, and indeed still are, very much a part of the London Anglo–Italian community, who organise a myriad of events such as dinner-dances, balls, barn dances and fund-raising dinners. But of all these events my favourite is the annual *scampagnata* which is a massive picnic that takes place in a field in the unfortunately-named village of Trotters Bottom, in Hertfordshire. (You couldn't make this stuff up if you tried.)

Annually on one Sunday in June, hundreds of Italians from all over London wend their way to Trotters Bottom where they assemble for a mass picnic en famille. Of course, this being an Italian picnic there is nary a sausage roll in sight and everyone tries to outdo each other, thus each year the picnics (and I use the word loosely) become more and more elaborate. Recently, I kid you not, one family showed up with a portable co vection oven containing a full Sunday roast with all the trimmings, including that most vital of picnic components, a candelabra.

On these occasions my mother tries hard to show a little restraint, although in the face of such blatant one-upmanship it's tough. Thus, year-by-year our own picnics become a little grander, despite my father keeping a keen eye on what Mum puts in the boot of the car so that he can take out what he deems inappropriate when her back is turned.

Torta di Patate is a bit of *scampagnata* tradition and the womenfolk vie with each other to see who produces the best 'torta'. Signore and Signorine, lay down your wooden spoons, my mum's got you beaten hands down and has done for the past 20 years. Here is her recipe, though even when I follow it to the letter it's never quite as good as hers.

Torta di Patate

1kg (2lb 4oz) onions, finely chopped; 50ml (2fl oz) extra virgin olive oil; 3kg (6½lb) King Edward potatoes cooked in their skins; 200g (7oz) sieved tinned tomatoes; 100g (4oz) grated Parmesan; 100g (4oz) grated Pecorino (if you don't have Pecorino use double the amount of Parmesan); 1 egg yolk; freshly ground salt and pepper.

Pastry: 225g (8oz) plain flour; 2 tbsp virgin olive oil; 2 whole eggs; salt and cold water.

Preheat the oven to 180°C (350°F). In a heavy-bottomed saucepan heat the oil on a low heat and sweat the onions until very soft. Add the sieved tomatoes and simmer gently for 15 minutes, adding a bit of stock made with a Kallo stock cube if it becomes too dry.

Peel the potatoes and mash with 60g (2½oz) of butter, then add the onion mixture, the Parmesan and Pecorino and the egg yolk, stir and season with freshly ground salt and pepper to taste.

Make the pastry by mixing the flour, eggs, oil and salt and add water to produce a stiff dough. Using a pasta machine or a heavy rolling pin, roll the pastry very thinly and line several oiled baking trays, allowing the pastry to overlap by half an inch all the way round. Spoon the mashed potato about 1in deep over the pastry base then fold the overlapping pastry around the edges and brush with beaten egg. Place in the centre of the oven for 30 minutes until the torta is golden brown.

Must-Haves for a Good Picnic

A large blanket (definitely the non-itchy kind), as well as a cotton sheet to place over it while you eat, to ensure that your blanket is food- and spillage-free for the rest of the day.

An iPod with speakers.

Sunscreen, insect repellent and sunglasses.

A cork screw, a sharp knife and, if you're barbecuing, tongs and a long fork.

A camera or camcorder.

A change of clothes, just in case.

A football, backgammon set or a deck of cards. as well as a steamy novel from which you can read to each other.

A whole kitchen roll, wipes for sticky fingers and accidents and a big black bin liner for rubbish.

A desire to behave like children for the entire day.

I DON'T LIKE MONDAYS

Nobody Loves Me, Everybody Hates Me,
Think I'll Go and Eat Worms

> *Some mornings it just doesn't seem worth*
> *gnawing through the leather straps.*
>
> EMO PHILLIPS

 There are times – and it doesn't matter how loved up you are or how good life is – when you wake up on a Monday morning and feel fed up, fat and frankly pissed off with the entire world. You have pressed the snooze button so many times on the state-of-the-art alarm clock that the batteries are failing. It used to call your name in a supposedly soothing manner but now it sounds like a strangled cat and you would rather walk on hot coals than get out of your nice warm bed and have to face the world. Right now you hate *it* and everything *in it*.

So you stumble out of bed and open the curtains in an attempt at feeling less like a vampire, praying for a single ray of sunshine but instead being greeted by driving rain bouncing off the pavement and the sight of next door's cat decimating the bag of rubbish that, in a moment of total apathetic indolence, you left outside the back door rather than placing it in the wheelie bin at the bottom of the garden. The entire patio is now strewn with the rather sodden pages from the *News of the World* and the leftovers from Sunday lunch mixed with cat litter, baked beans and potato peelings.

Nice.

You feel like weeping, but if you start you're not sure that you'll ever be able to stop. In a valiant effort to cheer you up, your man sings the 'Little Donkey' song which usually never fails to make you smile; he sings in the same funny voice, trundles around on all fours giving a blinding performance of a donkey struggling up a hill, sings all the verses and even repeats the chorus 3 times at the end. Bless him.

You try to smile but you end up baring your teeth instead. He looks a little frightened and leaves the house rather too quickly, retreating to the safety of his office.

Maybe the above is slightly exaggerated (poetic licence and all that), but once in a while we all get the dreaded

Monday Morning Blues. These are the days when we don't want to be nice to anyone, in fact, we want to be as horrible as can be and stay at home watching *Trisha* and doing absolutely nothing. Unfortunately the Monday Blues invariably hit us when we've got back-to-back meetings, a lunchtime dental appointment and it's peeing down outside.

So instead we struggle through the day, willing the time to go by super-quick so we can get home, unwind in a hot bath and go to bed really early to read *Heat*, watch *EastEnders* and cuddle the cat, weeping quietly into his fur.

Except, just as we are leaving the office at 5.31 we get waylaid by our utterly boring and terribly efficient boss who clearly needs to get a *life*, thus finding ourselves strap-hanging on the Northern Line at 7.30pm following a brainstorming session about new water coolers.

Finally, after walking from the tube in the pouring rain, we're home. We open the door, tear off our coat and collapse in a little puddle on the floor, wet hair plastered to our head, raindrops dripping from our eyelashes. Or are they tears? Enough already, I want my mummy.

The kitchen door opens and there he is, the one we love. Brandishing a huge glass of wine and a big smile, he engulfs us with an enormous bear hug, not caring that he's gonna get wet too, strokes our rather soggy hair and whispers:

'Poor baby, cheer up, drink your wine, I've run you a bath, have a long soak and when you're done pop on your pyjamas and snuggle on the sofa. I've taped *EastEnders* and tonight I'm cooking dinner.'

Suddenly nothing seems so bad, you're back on 7th Heaven and feeling very snug and loved. This is the reason we all look for our very own Mr Right, because everybody needs somebody sometimes.

Just in case that doesn't happen, good food is the next best thing to chase away the Monday Blues.

Old-fashioned Fish Pie

Filling: 450g (1lb) haddock, cod or coley fillets; 300ml (10fl oz) milk; 1 bay leaf; 6 black peppercorns; 1 onion, thickly sliced.

Topping: 100g (4oz) butter; 6 tbsp plain flour; 150ml (5fl oz) single cream; 2 hard-boiled eggs, roughly chopped; 3 tbsp finely chopped parsley; 100ml (4fl oz) milk; 800g (1¾lb) potatoes, cooked and mashed; 100g (4oz) butter; 100g (4oz) grated cheddar cheese; freshly ground salt and pepper.

Pre-heat the oven to 180°C (350°F). Place the fish in a shallow pan, pour over the milk and add the bay leaf, peppercorns, onion slices and salt to taste. Bring to the boil over a low heat and simmer for 6–8 minutes until the fish flakes when tested with a fork. (The thinner the fillets the less time you should cook them.) Lift the fish out of the milk using a slotted spoon, set aside then strain the milk through a fine sieve ensuring there are no peppercorns or fish bones floating around. Melt the butter in a saucepan, stir in the flour and cook gently on a low heat to form a smooth paste. Whisk in the reserved milk, stirring constantly as the sauce thickens.

Flake the fish into largish chunks and mix with the cream and parsley. Spoon the mixture into a shallow oven-proof dish and top with the béchamel sauce and a layer of chopped egg.

Heat the remaining milk and butter in a saucepan, remove from the heat and beat it into the mashed potato with the grated cheese. Season well with salt and pepper then spread over the top of the pie. Roughen up the surface of the potato with a fork, sprinkle with a grinding of black pepper and place in the centre of the oven for 30 minutes until bubbling and golden. Serve with peas and a great big cuddle.

There, there; tuck in, you'll start to feel better in no time at all.

WELCOME TO LOLA'S

Welcome to the Pleasure Dome

*How old would you be if you didn't know
how old you were?*

ANON

It's his birthday, his first birthday since you
moved in together and it's got to be special.

I have a real aversion to going out for celebratory meals,
I hate the feeling that one is obliged to go to a restaurant for
birthdays, anniversaries or, heaven help us, Valentine's
Night, that most excruciating of evenings which, in my
humble opinion, is the worst offender. It's dismal; rows and
rows of couples sat in lines of tightly-packed tables-for-
two, all eating the same supper from identical dreary
set-menus, all with the same sickly heart-shaped pudding,

surrounded by bouquets of overpriced, sub-standard, and by now wilting, red roses with Celine Dion warbling painfully in the background. I can't think of anything less romantic, except perhaps joint colonic irrigation.

Going 'out to dinner' for a special occasion always feels to my mind rather contrived. I like to go out as the mood takes me, rather than because I feel I 'should'. I like dining out to be a spontaneous event, rather than something I have to plan.

I'm aware that this means I won't always gain entry to those stellar, super-trendy restaurants where you have to book six months in advance, give your credit card number and pledge your first-born child to be waited on by staff kitted out in Prada, but hey, that's ok, because frankly I have no interest in going to a restaurant where the staff are better dressed than the customers and I am made to feel that they are doing me a favour by allowing me to eat there.

To that end I think birthday dinners should be intimate, indulgent affairs with lots of surprises so that the birthday boy/girl ends up feeling thoroughly spoilt and pampered.

Right, let's get back to the subject in hand, *his* birthday. We are going to make sure it's one he will never forget.

Start off as you mean to go on. I'm going to assume it's a weekday and therefore a workday.

Get up super early, tiptoe to the kitchen and prepare him a Birthday Breakfast in Bed. May I suggest that *before* you do this you make sure you look ok; serving him breakfast looking like a train wreck somewhat detracts from the experience. I'm not for one moment suggesting you spend hours getting all gussied up, just tidying up that bed-monster hair and adding a touch of blusher and a slick of lip gloss can make a hell of a difference at 7am. Also, shed the Paddington Bear pyjamas in favour of a sexy little nightdress.

Birthday Breakfast in Bed

A big fat kiss

Freshly-squeezed Orange Juice

More kisses

Coffee

*Scrambled Eggs and Smoked Salmon
and Wholegrain Toast*

Fresh Strawberries

Lots of cuddles

An Invitation to a VIP evening at Lola's

Clearly you'll need to shop for this the day before but that's no great hardship. We'll get to the invitation in a minute.

Everybody has their own way of making scrambled eggs, personally, I like mine with just butter, no milk. Once the butter is foaming in the saucepan over a gentle heat stir in the eggs with a wooden spoon and keep stirring. Remove the pan from the hob whilst the eggs are still soft and beat in a large knob of butter to halt the cooking process. I add salt at the end rather than the beginning as otherwise I think it toughens the eggs.

The rest of the breakfast treat just needs arranging on a tray. Don't forget to put a flower in a little vase and, whilst you're at it, an extra cup for yourself. I thought about including a bottle of champagne, but who in their right mind wants to drink champers at 7.30am on a school day? Best save it for later.

Now for the invitation.

We all have a secret wild side. A devil in a red dress. An alter ego. Mine is a little minx called Lola and I suggest for the purpose of this exercise you dig deep inside yourself, find *your* naughty girl and christen her. Everybody has a Lola, what's yours called?

Lola is quite a gal. She's a total hedonist; she loves to dance, is wholly self-assured and a total temptress. She dresses just like a woman should, loves to please her man and is flirty, feisty, fun, sexy and just a touch sultry. Oh, and she's a fabulous cook.

She's also an absolute whiz at birthdays.

Ok, you get the idea. Now that you've found your inner courtesan and named her, it's time for the invite. On a stiff piece of white card in your fanciest loopy writing (using a fountain pen not a biro), write to the birthday boy inviting him to dinner.

It should look something like this:

THE PLEASURE OF YOUR COMPANY
IS REQUESTED THIS EVENING AT

LOLA'S

IN ORDER TO CELEBRATE THE
JOYOUS OCCASION OF YOUR BIRTH

COCKTAILS 8PM
DRESS: BLACK TIE
CARRIAGES AT DAWN

Place the invitation in a white envelope and put it on the breakfast tray. No pressies until tonight – anticipation is everything. Wake him up with the Big Fat Kiss and serve him breakfast.

(Just for the record, as it's his birthday first there can be no excuses when it comes to yours; a last-minute card and beaten up chrysanthemums from the garage on the corner just won't cut *le moutarde*.)

When he reads the invitation and throws you a questioning look don't give the game away. Just tell him you have a surprise for him and try to look enigmatic. Sort of like the Mona Lisa, but less clenched.

After breakfast (and any other shenanigans), see him off to work with a cheery wave. I forgot to mention that, unbeknownst to him, you have the day off to prepare for tonight, but don't panic, everything you need is right here.

Tonight *you* are going to be his birthday present, his ultimate fantasy woman in the guise of Lola; the way she looks, her clothes, her make-up and her sassy, mischievous, shameless attitude are going to drive him crazy – and that's just for starters.

Don't dress too tartily, the look you are going for is indescribably wanton but not a total slut; a chaste, dissolute maiden rather than dissipated and depraved streetwalker.

As you are in your own home you can go a little mad and experiment with a brazen new look. If you always wear your hair down, put it up and vice versa; you need to look a little special, a little different and a lot raunchy. I suggest smoky eye shadow, red lipstick and the usual suspects – high heels and lots of perfume.

*The difference between pornography
and erotica is lighting.*

GLORIA LEONARD

The next thing we need to do is create an atmosphere of licentious and wicked abandonment, a sort of French brothel circa 1920 named after your inner temptress, in my case, Lola's.

The first thing he should see as he walks in the door is an overhead banner:

WELCOME TO LOLA'S, WHERE YOUR
PLEASURE IS MY PLEASURE

Time to tart the place up: concentrate on the dining room, the bathroom and the bedroom. Drape lots of scarves and throws over the furniture, light masses of candles (the idea is not to use any electric light whatsoever), have incense burning in every room, a bottle of champagne in a bucket full of ice, the table beautifully laid, rose petals strewn on clean white sheets and lots more candles in the bathroom (where you should run a bath for him, scattered with rose petals and essential oils, just before he gets home).

Music is key when trying to create a mood of dissolute immorality. I suggest a mix of Billie Holiday, Edith Piaf, Leonard Cohen (no one is more dissolute than Leonard Cohen), with perhaps some haunting Spanish guitar.

Don't blast it, it's supposed to be background music, as evocative and captivating as you are.

The food should be similar to a seduction dinner, nothing too heavy but luxurious and beautifully presented. The obvious thing to do would be to make one of his favourite dishes, something you know he'll love, but I prefer to dwell in the spirit of the evening and do something a little different that I haven't cooked before. The following menu is one I tried and tested on a recent Lola night. All I can tell you is, it worked.

I like to write a proper menu and place it on the table for occasions such as this. Again, it's just a matter of some stiff white card, loopy handwriting and a little imagination.

Happy Birthday to My Wonderful Man

Date: 19th August 2005
Venue: Lola's

Moules Marinières
Scampi Provençal
Saffron Rice
Green Leaf Salad
Birthday Surprise

It goes without saying that champagne should be served throughout the meal as it marries fantastically with everything and imparts a certain sense of occasion.

Moules Marinières

There are literally hundreds of versions of this recipe, some that strain and thicken the sauce, those that advise throwing away the empty half-shells and others where you are told to throw away half the sauce in case of a little stray grit from mussels.

Hogwash.

I once ate this in Marseilles out of a tin bucket in a small family restaurant in the port – they were the best mussels I have ever eaten. The lady of the house did all the cooking and she eschewed all the above fussing and fretting, and so do I. This is a rustic dish so don't be afraid to keep it just so.

There are, however, two golden rules. When cleaning the mussels discard any that are broken or cracked and any that are open and refuse to close when given a sharp tap with a knife. Conversely, when they are cooked discard any mussels that have not opened and remain tightly closed.

1kg (2lb 4oz) mussels scrubbed, washed, de-bearded and rinsed 4 times in cold water; 50g (2oz) butter; 2 shallots, finely chopped; 2 fat cloves of garlic, crushed and finely chopped; 300ml (10fl oz) white wine; 4 tbsp finely chopped parsley; 50ml (2fl oz) double cream; freshly ground salt and pepper.

In a wide-bottomed pot large enough to take all the mussels, melt the butter over a gentle heat, soften the onion and garlic then pour in the white wine and bring to the boil. Tip in the mussels and cover the saucepan, raising the heat a little. Leave to bubble for 4 minutes but shake the pan regularly to move everything around. Remove the lid, lift out the open mussels and place in a large warmed tureen (a slotted spoon is best for this). Remember to throw away any mussels that have not opened during cooking.

Once all the mussels have been removed from the pot, simmer the remaining liquor whilst whisking in the cream, a small knob of butter, the parsley and plenty of freshly ground black pepper. Pour the sauce over the mussels and serve immediately with a warm French baguette.

Scampi Provençal
This is very much a retro dish that I single-handedly want to resurrect in much the same way that posh chefs have been reinventing the Prawn Cocktail.

Scampi Provençal is magnificently pungent and garlicky, a real favourite of mine. As a precocious six-year-old my dad used to take my sister and me to the then-very-upmarket Manzi's Restaurant, in Leicester Square. I refused to eat anything else there (apart from the odd Dover Sole which I could de-bone unaided by the age of eight).

Scampi is the Italian name for Dublin Bay prawns –

these are actually miniature lobsters. If you can't find these in the shops then large prawns will do the trick, although they are slightly less sweet.

450g (1lb) scampi; 1 onion; 1 clove garlic; 30ml (1oz) olive oil; 100g (4oz) butter; 400g (14oz) chopped tinned tomatoes; 150ml (5fl oz) white wine; 1 tsp sugar; freshly ground salt and pepper.

Heat the oil in a heavy-bottomed pan and gently fry the onion and garlic until soft. Pour in the wine and reduce by half, add the tomatoes, sugar and check for seasoning then allow to simmer gently for 20 minutes.

Shell the scampi and in a separate pan melt the butter and cook until just pink. Add the scampi and the pan juices to the garlicky tomato sauce, stir well and bring to the boil. Serve immediately with some plain boiled rice cooked with a few strands of saffron and a tossed green salad dressed simply with balsamic vinegar and olive oil.

Birthday Surprise
You can't have a birthday without a birthday cake, it's just not right.

It's up to you what you do but, with only two people to eat it and with everything else that has to be done, I cheat and buy a beautifully-made cake. I'm not suggesting you grab a Mr Kipling Fondant Fancy and stick a household candle in it, I was thinking of a more exclusive French patisserie confection with proper birthday candles, accompanied by the whole 'put the lights out' routine where you sing Happy Birthday à la Marilyn Monroe to President Kennedy.

So that's everything you need for a Lola night. Except there is one more thing to set the tone of the evening as soon as your beloved gets home . . . Lay a trail of rose petals from the front door with a note telling him to follow them; at the end of the trail he will find you lounging seductively on the rose-strewn sheets, looking utterly seductive and just a little bit mysterious in the flickering candlelight with a warm welcome, two glasses of champagne and his birthday pressies.

I know it's corny and I know we've all seen it in the movies but, it's kinda cute and he'll be secretly chuffed that you made so much effort.

After dinner I suggest you play your favourite smoochy song and have a slow dance . . . after that, it's up to you what you do with the rest of the night, but I bet he's a very happy boy in the morning.

LA FAMIGLIA

The Heartbeat of our Lives

When I was a boy of fourteen, my father
was so ignorant I could hardly stand to have
the old man around. But when I got to be twenty-one,
I was astonished at how much he had learned
in seven years.

MARK TWAIN

Families. Love 'em or hate 'em they are a part of us and now and then it's nice for everyone to get together. I'm quite sure you have already met each other's parents, but it's unlikely that they have met each other or that you are acquainted with all the various siblings and grandparents.

If the very thought of getting both sets of family together

fills you with dread, don't do it. If you know they won't get on, it's a recipe for disaster. But in my world, that's unthinkable.

I believe Italians are genetically programmed to generate and endure family repasts and, even though they are often confrontational and raucous, I secretly love it when everyone gets together even if it can get a little noisy on occasion.

Introducing both families to each other means one thing and one thing only: Sunday Lunch.

> *Remember, as far as anyone knows we're*
> *a nice normal family.*
> HOMER SIMPSON

Growing up in an Italian household meant that there was simply no excuse for missing Sunday Lunch, and that still holds true today. *La famiglia* sitting down for a lovingly-prepared, leisurely meal is a long-held tradition and one that I hope, certainly in my own family, will never die.

When I'm travelling, Sunday is the one day of the week I am guaranteed to get horribly homesick and nostalgic over the Sunday lunches of my childhood. However, they were not always idyllic and at times they were far from tranquil; you can be sure that if there was a contentious issue best avoided it would surface somewhere between courses and would invariably lead to what could best be described as a 'lively debate'. The problem was, in typical

Italian style, our 'lively debates' sounded exactly like arguing, but as soon as dessert hit the table everyone piped down and harmony was once again restored. Until, that is, the ensuing fight over the washing-up.

Happy days.

Imagine both your families sitting round the table enjoying a wonderful meal and some good wine, joining together to celebrate your happiness and meeting the people that are so important to you both. What a lovely way to spend a Sunday.

I come from a typical family. You know, me, my mother, her third husband, his daughter from a second marriage, my stepsister, her illegitimate son.

CAROL HENRY

You are going to be catering for anywhere from 6 to 12 people (maybe more depending on the size of your respective families, the quantities in these recipes cater for 8 people), so make something that can be prepared in advance and that won't require too much attention. Go for a simple starter but produce a really spectacular pudding.

Get some decent wine and make sure the table looks nice. Treat your families like VIPs and make them feel special, then once they're lulled into a false sense of security it's so much easier to pounce on them and beg for that loan you need to finish the shower room!

LA FAMIGLIA

Traditional Family Sunday Lunch

STARTER

*Roasted Loin of Pork with Very Crispy Crackling
and Apple Sauce*

Crunchy Roast Potatoes with Rosemary and Garlic

Petits Pois à la Française

Chocolate and Raspberry Roulade

Roasted Loin of Pork with Very Crispy Crackling and Apple Sauce

A classic dish for Sunday lunch which needs no extra frills or fancy sauces. This is a spectacularly successful way to get really crunchy crackling.

2.5kg (5lb) loin of pork, boned and rolled with rind on; 100g (4oz) butter; coarse sea salt; 6 cloves of garlic; 12 small bay leaves; a glass of medium white wine.

Apple Sauce: 450g (1lb) cooking apples, peeled, cored and sliced; 30g (1¾oz) butter; 50g (2oz) sugar.

Get your butcher to bone, roll and tie your loin and have it deeply scored at ½in intervals. Preheat the oven to

205

220°C (425°F). For a really crisp crackling, place the joint skin-side down in a roasting tin and pour in boiling water to the depth of 1in. Place the pork in the centre of the oven and cook for 15 minutes. Remove from the oven, pour off the liquid and set aside to be used for basting. Melt the butter in the roasting pan and generously rub the skin of the loin with the coarse salt, then insert garlic cloves and bay leaves into the score marks. Roast the loin skin-side up at 180°C (350°F), at 30 minutes for every 500g (1lb). Baste every 30 minutes. When cooked, allow the meat to rest for 10 minutes and then remove the pan and keep warm. Drain the fat from the roasting tray and place over a low flame on the hob. Deglaze the tray with a glass of wine, allowing it to bubble and thicken and making sure you scrape the burnt bits into the gravy.

Put the apples in a saucepan with 50ml (2fl oz) of water and cook gently, uncovered, until soft. Beat with a wooden spoon until puréed and pass through a sieve. Return to the pan and stir in the butter and the sugar. Serve warm.

Crunchy Roast Potatoes with Rosemary and Garlic

I am a roast potato fiend and was always proud of my seemingly successful roast spuds, crunchy on the outside and fluffy on the inside, until I tried my sister's. Hers proved to be even crunchier and much, much fluffier.

I adhere to the same old Delia trick of boiling, shaking then roasting as my sister, except she shallow fries them betwixt shaking and roasting. Slightly more time consuming, but worth every minute.

2kg (4½lb) floury potatoes, peeled and cut into large chunks; the ideal oil for roasting is duck or goose fat, but failing that sunflower oil; coarse salt; a large handful fresh rosemary needles; 10 unpeeled cloves of garlic.

Place the potatoes in a saucepan of cold, salted water and parboil for 7 minutes. Drain, put back in the saucepan and give 'em a good old shake until the outside of the potatoes are somewhat roughed up. Keeping the lid on, set them aside whilst you heat about ½in of fat in an oven tray on the hob with half the rosemary leaves. When the fat is very hot, tip in the potatoes, turning them so they are well coated in oil, and cook on the hob until the potatoes are golden brown. Scatter with the rest of the rosemary and the garlic cloves and cook in the oven at 200°C (400°F) for an hour.

Petits Pois à la Française

450g (1lb) frozen petits pois; 6 tbsp butter; 1 small gem lettuce, shredded; 5 spring onions, chopped; 2 tsp sugar; a handful of chopped flat leaf parsley; salt and freshly ground pepper.

Melt the butter in a saucepan and stir in all the ingredients along with 50ml (2fl oz) of boiling water. Simmer with the lid on for 15 minutes until the peas are tender. Season with salt and pepper and sprinkle with the parsley.

Chocolate and Raspberry Roulade

(This serves 8 but that's only one piece each and you will definitely want more than that! For 8 people, make two.)

Sponge: 6 large eggs, separated; 150g (5oz) sugar; 50g (2oz) dark cocoa powder.

Filling: 225g (8oz) plain chocolate, 70 per cent cocoa solids; 2 tbsp water; 2 large eggs, separated; 225ml (8fl oz) double cream, whipped; 2 punnets fresh raspberries; icing sugar.

Preheat the oven to 180°C (350°F) and line an oiled baking tray with silicone paper. Make the filling first. Melt the chocolate in a bowl over a saucepan of simmering water. Remove from the heat and whisk until smooth. Whisk 2 egg yolks in a separate bowl and then add them to the warm chocolate mixture. Let it cool for a bit then, in another bowl, whisk the 2 egg whites until stiff and fold them into the chocolate mixture. Put it in the fridge for about an hour.

Meanwhile, make the sponge. Whisk the 6 egg yolks until they start to thicken, add the caster sugar and continue whisking until it thickens a little more before adding the cocoa powder. In a separate bowl, whisk the egg whites until they form soft peaks then carefully fold them into the egg yolk mixture. Pour the whole thing into the prepared cake tin. Bake on the centre shelf for 20–25 minutes until risen and springy to the touch. Take it out of the oven and allow it to cool before you remove it from the tin.

When cool, turn the tray out onto a piece of grease-proof paper that has been liberally sprinkled with icing sugar. Peel away the silicone paper from the bottom of the cake (which is now facing upwards) and spread it with the chocolate mousse filling, followed by the whipped cream. Scatter with a thin layer of fresh raspberries on top.

Finally, very gently roll up the cake to make a log; the cake will crack in places, but that's a good thing as it looks really pretty.

HOME ALONE

☙

Ferris Bueller's Day Off

Please go away so I can miss you.

ANON

As you settle into the day-to-day routine of your lives together, at some point it's highly likely that one of you will be away from home for a few nights (either on business or on a weekend with the boys/girls), thus leaving the other one home alone for the first time in months and months.

How fantastic!

Don't take that the wrong way, as much as we love sharing and caring for our man, there is nothing quite like a few days apart safe in the knowledge that it's temporary and that the reunion will be hot, hot, hot!

Sure, we're gonna miss him, but you know what they say? Distance makes the heart grow ever so much fonder, meanwhile it gives us the opportunity to kick back and spend a few days doing exactly what we want to do, completely spoiling and utterly pampering ourselves.

I love it when I have a few days just for myself, preferably over a long weekend. I tearfully wave my man goodbye, double-lock the front door behind me and feel for all the world as though I'm auditioning for the role of Ferris Bueller in said movie.

(Just in case you missed it, Ferris Bueller is a teenage boy who plays truant for a day by acting sick and manages to wreak all kinds of havoc without getting caught by his parents – despite their concerned visits. It's terrifying the damage that a crafty teenager can do in 48 hours.)

I can watch all the trashy TV I want, including the reality shows and soaps that drive my man nuts. I can spend hours and hours in the bath with Marvin Gaye crooning to me whilst sipping a glass of icy champagne as I catch up with all my girlfriends over the phone, including those in Australia, New York and Singapore and, best of all, I can go shopping and return laden with bags without having to hide them in the hall closet before he sees them.

Childish? Yes. Tragic? Absolutely. But, unfortunately, all true.

As I mentioned earlier in the book I love cooking for

myself. Some people think that's a little weird and something that one shouldn't admit to, rather like a dirty secret one would air on an episode of *Jerry Springer*, but I get as much pleasure cooking solely for me as I do cooking for others. I can be as creative as I want, I get a free hand with the chilli, I can pig out in private and, what's more, I get to do it in my pyjamas watching anything I choose to on TV. It doesn't get any better than that.

During my solitary weekends I love catching up with friends and family but I always reserve one evening for me and me alone, observing the old adage 'Ain't no one going out, ain't no one coming in'. I tend to catch up with my mates on Friday nights (the best night of the week for partying) and then see my family for, yes, you guessed it, Sunday lunch. Which leaves a blissful Saturday all to myself.

The day starts as I wake up around 10am and have coffee in bed watching the Saturday morning cookery shows. After a quick shower I take myself out for brunch, which is generally Eggs Benedict at Café Laville in Little Venice where you will find me tucked away at a corner table overlooking the canal, relishing my solitude over a good book.

(It's a strange anomaly of life that the solitude of eating out alone when you are normally part of a twosome can be stimulating and slightly exciting, whereas eating out alone when it's the norm can be just plain lonely.)

After brunch I mooch around for a bit, visiting the odd book shop and doing a bit of clothes shopping, but the latter part of the afternoon is reserved for Selfridges Food Hall where I buy the one thing I know my boyfriend can't bear to look at but which I simply adore – jellied eels.

Don't knock it until you've tried it. I have bastardised the traditional malt vinegar philosophy and I choose to eat my eels with finely chopped fresh chillies, a sprinkling of coriander, a little lemon juice and freshly ground salt and pepper. My father, being an eel and malt vinegar purist, will probably disown me upon reading this.

I also buy anything else I fancy, as it is my intention to have a night alone with my own private feast and the remote control.

I tend to go for easy-to-prepare food and I must admit to having a penchant for the usual stuff such as pasta and risotto, but on 'Ferris' evenings such as these I also revert to the trailer-trash food slut that I really am and find myself yearning for pies, chips and the odd takeaway. However, as these detract from the pleasure of cooking I tend not to give in to these primal and rather grubby urges.

On my last 'home alone' weekend I devoured my beloved jellied eels followed by my cheat's version of Thai Prawn Curry served with Jasmine Rice and steamed Pak-Choi. It's easy to prepare, really yummy and quite healthy – shame that I then had to ruin it later by devouring 3 Krispy Kreme Donuts whilst watching *100 Best TV*

Shockers on Channel 5. (Just for the record, it's all true, Krispy Kreme are totally scrumptious, so much so that I had the fourth one for breakfast on Sunday. Thankfully, these are a bi-annual treat as I dread to think how many calories they actually contain.)

A Thai-ish Prawn Curry

I would love to tell you that I grind my own spices, make my own curry paste and cream my own coconuts, but the truth is that I don't. You can buy some excellent Thai products these days, although the supermarkets still have a long way to go in terms of Thai herbs and spices. Thai holy basil is glorious, totally unlike European basil with a flavour that is impossible to replicate. Tom Yum stock cubes or Tom Yum paste are an essential part of bastardising real Thai cuisine in your own kitchen and neither of these, as yet, seems to be available on the high street.

If you live in London I recommend a trip to Chinatown for your Asian herbs such holy basil, coriander, kaffir lime leaves, fresh mint, curry leaves, lemon grass and Thai ginger – galangal – there they are sold in large bundles at a fraction of the price of the ones you get in supermarkets. (You know the ones, minuscule amounts of herbs packed in annoying plastic envelopes sold at an absurdly expensive price.) Other great buys are big bottles of sweet chilli sauce, tamarind, Kikkoman soy sauce and lots of other Chinese condiments – often at half the price of regular stores. Chinatown is a fabulous shopping experience, check out the frozen prawns while you're there, they're exceptionally good value. If you don't live in London, keep an eye out for an authentic Chinese grocery store near you, or log on to www.chinatown-online.co.uk and find your nearest store through their directory of Britain.

(This recipe will serve two normal people or one greedy one.)

6–8 large prawns, uncooked, shelled; 3 tbsp Thai red curry paste; 1in ginger, finely sliced; 1 garlic clove, finely sliced; 1 stick lemon grass, bashed up and bruised; 2 kaffir lime leaves, ripped in half; a large handful finely chopped coriander; a large handful holy basil (if you can get it); 1 large, red, mild chilli, finely sliced; 1 spring onion, finely sliced; 3 tbsp fish sauce; 30ml (1½fl oz) lime juice; 30ml (1½fl oz) sweet chilli sauce; 300ml (10fl oz) chicken stock, from a cube; 2 tbsp coconut cream.

In a heavy-bottomed pan gently fry the curry paste with the ginger, garlic, chilli, spring onion, lime leaves and half the coriander and holy basil. When sizzling, add the fish sauce, sweet chilli sauce and the hot stock, bring to a simmer then add the coconut cream. Test for heat, if it's too hot add a little more coconut or if it's not hot enough, a touch more curry paste. The sauce should have the consistency of thin cream, if it's too dry add water, if too thin, reduce it a little. Add the prawns and simmer for around 5 minutes until cooked. Stir in the rest of the coriander and basil.

I am aware that this is not terribly authentic but nonetheless it tastes wonderful. Serve it with some plain, steamed jasmine rice and steamed pak-choi or choi sum which are both readily available in most supermarkets, but which are considerably fresher and cheaper in Chinatown or Asian stores.

IN SICKNESS AND IN HEALTH

❦

Let's Play Doctors and Nurses

*The art of medicine consists in amusing the patient
whilst nature effects a cure.*

VOLTAIRE

 Oh dear, oh dear, oh dear! One of you is not feeling very well, huh? There, there.

It is hard not to snicker as I write this. Now is the time you really get the measure of the person you are shacked up with. Yes, boys and girls, that's right, it's time for real-life doctors and nurses. (Minus the kinky outfits and the sex.)

I'm bursting to say something that I would love to have the restraint to withhold; I yearn to possess the self-control that brings with it that rare gift, diplomacy. But I don't, so here goes.

In my experience and, yes, I'm sure there are exceptions to this rule: men are crap, really crap, at being ill. And just to make things worse, they are not so hot at doing the looking after when someone else is ill. They do try, but when you're already feeling poorly and the person that is looking after you doesn't know the difference between cough medicine and syrup of figs (true story), your patience tends to dissipate fairly quickly.

I promise I'm not having a go at men, but they truly don't have the nurturing gene. It's not their fault God in her infinite wisdom just decided that women would be better at it. She was right.

> *The last time I saw anything like you*
> *the whole herd had to be destroyed.*
>
> ERIC MORECAMBE

The other problem is that when men have a cold it's never just a cold it's 'da flu'. Anyone who has ever really had 'da flu' (i.e. your actual influenza), will know that you are as good as dead for about 10 days. You literally cannot move, cannot speak and certainly cannot watch TV whilst demanding boiled egg and soldiers and complaining that your throat hurts so much but perhaps you could manage just one more bowl of cereal, oh, and by the way, where's the newspaper?

Ok, back to the point in hand, one of you is poorly.

The upside of sharing a home is that there is someone to look after you, listen to your catalogue of aches and pains and make up a sick bed on the sofa complete with duvet and a pillow sprinkled with lavender oil for your poor little sore nose, that you pronounce *dose*. (Men, please take note, this is nurturing.) It also means you have someone to cook you get-well-soon food.

We've already mentioned soft-boiled eggs and soldiers, which in my mind is a real winner for poorly boys, but there are lots of other soothing comfort foods that will help us regain our strength in record time.

Being ill is one of the greatest pleasures in life,
provided one is not too ill and is not obliged
to work until one is better.

SAMUEL BUTLER

Under-the-weather foods need to be consoling, soothing and warming. I can't think of a single cold dish that fits the bill – except maybe cereal and even that tastes better with hot milk if someone is unwell.

Nursery food is brilliant if you're not feeling great. When I was a little girl and felt a bit poorly my grandfather would prepare for me an earthenware bowl full of hot milk sweetened with honey, into which he would break small pieces of bread cut from a large white country loaf. If it was a little stale, so much the better. The bread soaked up the milk and nothing in the world tasted as good or warmed my tummy better than his *zuppa*. It's a cuddle in a bowl.

Soup is also a brilliant 'feel-better' food. I love tomato soup with hot buttered toast and this is one of the few times that homemade just doesn't work. It has to be tinned and it has to be Heinz. Sorry, nothing, and I mean nothing, else will do. You can keep your sun-ripened tomato and basil concoctions for dinner parties. When I'm poorly I want Heinz . . . and unsalted butter on my soldiers . . . and make sure it's hot.

> *I feel the end approaching. Quick bring me my dessert, coffee and liqueur.*

> BRILLAT SAVARIN

Another throwback from my childhood is minestrina, which involves cooking *stelline*, tiny pasta stars, in homemade chicken stock with a grating of Parmesan to serve.

My father's cure-all, on the other hand, is boiling whole onions and garlic cloves with the contents of a bottle of red wine until they are soft, eat everything in the pot and then go to bed and sweat it out. Not convinced, Dad.

There is a Chinese remedy for all that ails you in the form of Congee. Add finely chopped spring onions, ginger and garlic to white rice that has been well rinsed then simmer everything in chicken stock until the rice has practically dissolved into the liquid. It takes about 2 hours from start to finish. I once watched a friend of mine go from 'unable to walk' at midday to 'let's party' by 9pm on the strength of a large bowl of Congee, 1 tequila shot, a new pair of Earl Jeans and sheer willpower.

Alex's Love Juice

Time for the mother of all restorative soups. This potion is guaranteed to get me back on my feet when all else has failed; it has been known to cure hangovers, broken hearts, toothache, earache, a sore foot, the common cold, gastric problems and even to pour oil on the troubled waters of a disagreement.

I truly believe it is impossible to be sad with a steaming bowlful of this fragrant nectar in front of you. I have yet to meet a person, male or female that didn't almost weep with pleasure when they first tasted this and, in fact, I have had some very passionate responses upon serving it, including one proposal of marriage and some far less formal and much naughtier suggestions.

Perhaps it's an aphrodisiac too?

The soup has had many incarnations, but most recently as Alex's Love Juice after a very good friend of mine commented that it seemed to bring a sense of wellbeing and peace to whomsoever partook of it.

Please don't be scared off by the long list of ingredients,

I promise you that it's easy to prepare and you will find yourself making it again and again.

It's hard to give the precise measurements for my Love Juice as it changes a little every time I make it. As I said in the Home Alone section, you can find Tom Yum stock cubes or paste and Thai holy basil in Asian supermarkets, whilst Laksa paste, kaffir lime leaves, lemon grass and coriander are now freely available in most supermarkets. If you don't have holy basil, don't worry, it tastes just as good without it, but please don't substitute ordinary basil as it just doesn't work. Vegetarians can leave out the chicken and use a vegetable stock and it tastes wonderful, in fact, sometimes even better as the flavours are more delicate.

Make sure all your chopping and slicing is done before you start making the soup so all you then have to do is combine everything.

1 litre (1¾ pints) chicken stock; 2 x Tom Yum stock cubes or 3 tbsp Laksa or Tom Yum paste; 1 tsp tamarind paste; 10ml 2 tsp Thai fish sauce; 150ml (5fl oz) Thai sweet chilli sauce; 2 large handfuls finely chopped fresh coriander; 2 stalks lemon grass, finely chopped; 2 large handfuls finely chopped Thai holy basil; 2 kaffir lime leaves, thinly sliced; 1 handful fresh mint, finely chopped; 2in piece of fresh ginger, very finely sliced; 2 cloves of garlic, very finely sliced; juice of 1 lemon; 300ml (10fl oz) coconut cream; 150g (5oz) roughly chopped mushrooms; 150g (5oz) bean sprouts; 3 spring onions,

chopped into ¼in rounds; 2 medium heads pak-choi; 2 medium
chicken breasts, sliced into ribbons; 200g (7oz) egg noodles,
cooked and drained.

Wash and chop all the ingredients as required. Cook the
noodles, refresh under cold water and set to one side.
Separate the white stems of the pak-choi from the leaves,
cut the stems into uniform 1in lengths and blanch in
boiling water until just tender. Roll up all the leaves and
shred thinly, set aside.

Bring the chicken stock to the boil and add the Tom
Yum cubes or Laksa paste, lemon juice, tamarind paste,
fish sauce, sweet chilli sauce, 1 handful of coriander,
1 handful of holy basil, all of the mint, the sliced ginger,
sliced garlic, kaffir lime leaves, mushrooms, lemon grass,
spring onions and coconut cream and simmer gently for
half an hour, skimming off any scum that may form on the
surface as it cooks.

Ten minutes before you want to serve the soup, add the
chicken strips and 8 minutes later add the bean sprouts.

The soup needs to be served in wide, deep bowls (8in x
6in Pyrex mixing bowls are perfect or, better yet, large
Chinese noodle bowls). Reheat the noodles briefly in hot
water and place a mound at the bottom of the bowl. Using
a slotted spoon, top with the mushrooms, chicken
ribbons, bean sprouts and other bits and bobs from the
soup. On top of that place the blanched pak-choi stems

and a few ribbons of the raw leaves and top the whole thing off with a large ladleful of the soup liquid. Garnish with a sprinkling of chopped coriander and basil.

This will look like a huge amount of food but I have never known anyone not to finish it or go back for seconds. I love to eat this with chopsticks and a Chinese spoon and it is absolutely de rigueur to slurp from the bowl at the end.

> *After two days in hospital I took a turn*
> *for the nurse.*
>
> W. C. FIELDS

Other than soups, eggs and milky things there probably isn't too much more you fancy when you are poorly, apart from lots of TLC, cuddles and some peace and quiet.

I love to snuggle up in bed wearing soft, fleecy pyjamas with fresh sheets and a downy comforter. If I feel up to it I'll read a trashy novel between naps and will be as quiet as a mouse. BUT (as usual with me there is, of course, a 'but'), I love lots of attention and silly little pressies, certainly some flowers and some magazines: *Heat*, *National Enquirer* and *Hello* and I might just about be able to manage some of those really nice, expensive Belgian chocolates.

(Ok, ok, maybe it's not just the men that like to milk it for all it's worth. I'm ready for my close up, Mr Spielberg!)

REALITY CHECK

~

Let's Play Doctors and Nurses

 So, when it comes right down to it, is he Mr Right or Mr Right Now?

It probably seems like a really surprising question to be asking at this stage in the relationship. For some of you, but for others?

Well, you've probably been expecting it, perhaps even flicking through the pages towards the back of this book looking for just such a notion. My point is this: you've been living together for a while and have come through the preliminary getting-to-know-you phase of sharing lives and it would seem that now, finally, you really are *getting-to-know-each-other*.

A number of you have never been happier and your love affair just keeps getting better, you both count your lucky stars at least once a day, genuflecting at the altar of the celestial force that brought you together. Being apart is just unthinkable. You have found the Holy Grail of modern-day romance, True Love, ergo, Mr Right.

Meanwhile, back at Checkpoint Reality, there are those of you who don't feel quite the same way even though you initially thought you did, might still do, or really want to.

Things are ok, but not quite as amazing as you thought they would be and whilst *you're* certainly not worshipping at any celestial altars, neither are you heading out the door. You want this to work and so, it seems, does he and even though nothing awful has happened you just seem to be a little further apart every day.

> *Hanging onto a bad relationship is like*
> *chewing gum after the flavour has gone.*
>
> RITA RUDNER

It could well be that you are in the grip of Romantic Love and not, as we dared hope, True Love. The cracks might be starting to show but, as we all know, relationships are never easy, in fact sometimes they're damn hard work, so it could just be that the time has come to go that extra mile. True Love *will* out, as will Romantic Love, and either way you shouldn't give up without a bloody good fight.

For some people The Middle lasts a lifetime as they spend eternity in 7th Heaven – getting married, having kids, forever and ever, amen – and even though life will throw the same crap at them as it does at everybody now and again, they'll come through it because when you are with 'the one' even the darkest of days are sustainable because, as we already know, True Love Conquers All.

For the rest of us, well, if he's not really 'the one' then no matter *what* we do eventually it will become painfully obvious as we watch our relationship slipping away from us, the harsh realities of its demise being played against a backdrop of broken dreams and 'what ifs?'

Ouch, I don't like this one little bit, I would rather still be cooking for all and sundry in The Middle or chatting excitedly about Soul Mates but, as we agreed earlier, modern-day relationships exist in the realm of The Beginning, The Middle and The End. For some of us The End might just be nigh and we can't have new Beginnings until we deal with the End.

> *The trouble with some women is they get all*
> *excited about nothing and then marry him.*
>
> CHER

I really don't want to rain on anyone's parade but if you're having doubts it's worth asking yourself a couple of brutally frank questions:

When you think about getting married (and, let's face it, every girl does), do you sit there gazing into space thinking how wonderful it would be to be his wife, bear his name and possibly even his children? Can you envisage growing old together, or is it the fabulous three-months'-salary sparkler, the one-of-a-kind designer gown, a far-flung exotic honeymoon and the idea of being a princess for the day that sets your heart fluttering?

Do you see your future as similar to that of Katharine Hepburn and Henry Fonda in the classic movie *On Golden Pond* or is it more Michael Douglas and Kathleen Turner in *The War of the Roses*?

Here comes the million-dollar question: if you knew then what you know now, would you have ever gone on that very first date?

We don't really get to know someone until we live with them and share the minutiae of our lives, our fears, our hopes and our dreams and whilst sometimes we like what we find and fall even more in love, there are times when just the reverse can happen. The problem arises when our initial perceptions of someone are incorrect and they turn out to be totally different to who we thought they were, and this slowly becomes more apparent as we get to know them better. It's no one's fault, you can't blame them for our ill-conceived expectations and we shouldn't expect or even want to change someone to suit our perceptions or our requirements.

I'm sure that there are some of you who, reading between the lines, will recognise this situation in your own relationships and understand exactly what I'm talking about even if, as yet, you are not ready to admit it to each other. And, of course, there will be those of you who don't have a clue what I'm talking about as your relationship is going from strength to strength and he is exactly who you thought he was. In fact, he's a million times more fantastic. Bully for you. Enjoy. The rest of us are heading for troubled waters but you know what they say: no pain, no gain.

Thus far, *Eat Me* has welcomed you to The Beginning and The Middle. I am not going to welcome you to The End, or pretend that it's going to be easy, but I can promise you a shoulder to cry on, helpful advice born of experience and lots of good food to help you through it.

PLAYLIST:

Sade: **No Ordinary Love**
Beyoncé: **Crazy in Love**
Diana and Marvin: **You are Everything**
Alicia Keys: **If I Ain't Got You**
Baby Bird: **You're Gorgeous**
Van Morrison: **Brown Eyed Girl**
Norah Jones: **Come Away With Me**
Dido: **Thank You**
Aretha Franklin: **Natural Woman**
Robert Palmer: **Addicted to Love**

THE END

I have discovered there is Romance in food when
Romance has disappeared from everywhere else.
And, as long as my digestion holds out,
I will follow Romance.

ERNEST HEMINGWAY

Oops, you're at it again, bickering over the silliest things even when you try really hard not to.

You wake up in the morning full of good intentions, promising yourselves that today there will be no stupid arguments over silly things like *who* forgot to put the phone on to charge, *who* had the last of the milk, *who* lost the car keys, *whose* turn it is to de-flea the cat; and so it continues. You know what I'm talking about; that petty, trivial, inconsequential stuff that has nothing at all to do with the real reason that you are at each other's throats. You're not ready to face that yet.

The good news is that you are both acutely aware that

these childish spats are eroding the very foundations of the bond you have forged and therefore you are both keen to make a concerted effort to stop the squabbling and back-biting. The bad news is, you don't seem to be able to.

Time to wave goodbye to 7th Heaven and as you do so you may notice a few storm clouds looming, heralded by the echo of distant, but fast-approaching, thunder. We have arrived at the nitty-gritty part of relationships, when we sort the wheat from the chaff and see if we have what it takes to make the grade.

Is it True Love? Or just a bloody good imitation?

Time to find out.

THUNDER & LIGHTNING

Run For Cover

Love and murder will out.
WILLIAM CONGREVE

Things may not be ideal and you may well be going through a sticky patch, but having come this far you *have* to give it your very best shot. And anyway, everyone, even the most loved up of couples, have ups and downs; nothing is picture-perfect all of the time and if we need to make a bit of an effort to try and get things back on track, then so be it.

I suggest you spend some time together doing things which you *both* enjoy and which used to be an intrinsic part of your relationship but which, lately, you have had neither the inclination nor the patience for.

I'm not talking about sex (although you should probably brush up on that as well if it ain't shakin' in the bedroom department). I'm talking about hobbies or shared interests, anything from hiking or bird-watching to taxidermy; it doesn't matter what it is as long as you find some common ground and stop bickering.

And in my world, that brings us nicely back to food.

At a critical time during the break-up of my marriage, New Year's Eve threatened to be a particularly painful affair. For a while we had been spending far too many evenings in front of the telly at separate ends of the sofa in a not-very-companionable silence or, worse, out on the town with friends, but not with each other. Despite this, we made a conscious decision to see the New Year in together in an attempt to re-kindle the embers of our failing relationship. Thus we decided to do what we had always done best – throw a party. So we arranged to host a New Year's Eve dinner for our closest friends.

As is the case in so many situations like ours we still loved each other, we just didn't seem to be able to connect anymore. We hoped that in organising and enjoying the party together, in finding some common ground, we would find each other again. We sent out 10 totally over-the-top invitations to our closest friends. Everyone was asked to dress up as their favourite Forties or Fifties movie star, and each couple was asked to bring not one but two bottles of champagne.

We provided everything else, of course, including those lovely intricate masks you see at Venetian Carnival Balls, party poppers, streamers, a lavish feast and, as was traditional, one of my killer cocktails.

We spent hours poring over cookbooks trying to work out the perfect menu to feed 12 people. It had to be something that would reek of luxury but would not break the bank, nor should it require us to spend the whole evening in the kitchen; thereby neglecting our guests and not allowing us to enjoy ourselves either.

Once we'd solved the challenge, we hand-wrote each menu so that everyone would have a keepsake of the evening.

EVENING EXTRAVAGANZA

DINE WITH THE STARS

Bellini Cocktails

Potage Saint-Germain

Rosti Potato with Smoked Salmon and Caviar

Boeuf en Croûte Watercress Salad

Chocolate Dacquoise

Marrons Glacés and Coffee

Bellini

This is a lovely combination of fresh peach juice and champagne and is very simple to make.

Peel and stone 10 fresh peaches and whizz them in the liquidiser. Quarter-fill a champagne glass with the juice and top it up with ice-cold champagne. Stir and serve.

(There are those who add a small measure of peach liqueur or schnapps, but I prefer it without.)

Potage Saint-Germain

A gorgeous dinner-party soup, pale green in colour and tasting exactly like spring. You could use fresh peas but frozen ones do the job just as well.

6 leeks; 1kg (2lb 4oz) frozen petits pois, defrosted; 2 butter lettuces; 3 litres (5 pints) vegetable stock, either your own or Marigold; 2 tbsp sugar; 1 handful chopped parsley; 1 handful chopped chervil; 4 tbsp butter; salt and freshly ground black pepper.

Trim the leeks and cut into ¼in slices, rinse well and drain. Heat 2 tablespoons of the butter in a large heavy-bottomed pan, add the leeks and cook gently until soft. Meanwhile shred the lettuce, then add it to the softened leeks with the peas, stock and sugar. Allow to simmer for 15 minutes. Remove from the heat, add half the parsley and chervil and whizz in a blender or food processor until smooth.

Just before serving heat the soup to a gentle simmer and whisk in the remaining butter. Serve with a sprinkling of parsley mixed with chervil.

Rosti Potato with Smoked Salmon and Caviar

This is a wonderfully opulent starter that makes a little bit of caviar go an awfully long way. I love the combination of hot rosti with ice-cold caviar and if you are making this for just the two of you (and you're feeling particularly flush), skip the smoked salmon altogether and pile on the caviar. For 12 people that is, perhaps, a little excessive.

1kg (2lb 4oz) potatoes; 2 eggs, beaten; 100ml (3½oz) olive oil; 200ml (7fl oz) sour cream; 100g (4oz) Iranian caviar; 100g (4oz) smoked salmon, cut into very fine, long ribbons; freshly ground salt and pepper.

Peel and boil the potatoes for about 10 minutes until cooked but still quite firm (you need to be able to grate them without them falling apart). Drain them and pop them into the fridge for at least 3 hours. When chilled, grate them on the large side of the grater into long, thin ribbons, add the beaten egg, 15ml (1 tbsp) of the oil and season with salt and pepper.

Heat some of the remaining oil in a large, heavy-bottomed, non-stick frying pan. Using 2 tablespoons of the potato mix at a time, cook over a medium heat. Fry on both sides until golden brown, pressing down gently on each cake with a fish slice. Remove from the pan when cooked and drain on kitchen paper. Keep going until you have finished all of the mix and have 12 potato cakes.

If you are cooking the rosti in advance pop them under the grill for a minute just before you are ready to serve them. Allow them to cool slightly then top with the sour cream, ribbons of smoked salmon and a spoonful of caviar.

Totally decadent, darling!

Boeuf en Croûte

An utterly extravagant, over the top, sumptuous and horribly expensive dish but, it is a special occasion and we are pulling out all the stops. Also, considering just how fabulous it is, it's spectacularly simple and can be finished off in the oven whilst you are having the starters. I suggest making 2 croûtes that will each feed 6.

2 packets frozen, ready-rolled puff pastry; 2 x 800g (1lb 12oz) thick-end of fillet of beef; 100g (4oz) butter; 2 onions, very finely chopped; 500g (1lb 2oz) button mushrooms, very finely chopped; 100g (4oz) dried porcini mushrooms,

soaked in 300mls (10fl oz) boiling water; 200g (7oz) butter;
100ml (3½fl oz) brandy; 2 eggs, beaten; salt and freshly
ground black pepper.

Preheat oven to 190°C (375°F). Trim the meat, removing
any visible fat or sinews, and rub all over with half the
butter and some brandy. Place the meat in a roasting tin
and cook for 30 minutes, basting now and again with
more brandy and the juices from the meat. Remove from
the oven and leave to rest.

To make the mushroom duxelles (the mushroom paste),
drain the porcini mushrooms and chop very finely. Melt
the remaining butter in a heavy-bottomed pan, add the
onion and cook over a gentle heat until soft then add the
button and porcini mushrooms. Continue to cook for
20 minutes until all the liquid from the mushrooms has
evaporated. When the mixture is dry, throw the rest of the
brandy into the pan and let it sizzle for a couple of
minutes. Season well with salt and pepper and allow it to
cool thoroughly.

When both the meat and the mushroom duxelles are
cold, cut 2 pieces of pastry in rectangles approximately
35 x 25cm each. Spread a quarter of the mushroom
duxelles over the centre portion of each pastry piece in
approximately the same shape and size as the meat. Place
the beef fillet on top of the mushroom duxelles and cover
with the remaining mixture, patting it down. Brush the

edges of the pastry with a beaten egg and wrap the pastry around the meat like a parcel, making sure the edges are well sealed.

Place the parcel on an oiled oven tray and keep covered in a cool place until you are ready to cook. Just before you sit down to enjoy your soup, brush both pastry parcels with beaten egg and place in a hot oven: 230°C (450°F) for 30 minutes.

Just before serving, make a gravy with the juices from the meat and add a little more brandy and stock if necessary. Carve at the table into thick slices and serve with a simple watercress salad dressed with a little olive oil and red wine vinegar.

Chocolate Dacquoise

This confection actually tastes of celebration and other than the fact that it is so gorgeous, the best thing about it is that it can be made well in advance and assembled on the day.

Meringue: 100g (4oz) finely ground hazelnuts; 250g (9oz) caster sugar; 2 tbsp cornflour; 7 egg whites; a pinch of cream of tartar; 2 drops white wine vinegar; 4 drops vanilla essence; ½ cup roasted, crushed hazelnuts.

Filling: 450ml (15fl oz) double cream; 500g (1lb 2 oz) 70 per cent cocoa solids dark chocolate, broken up into small pieces; 50ml (2fl oz) brandy; icing sugar for dusting.

You will need a piping bag and a 1cm nozzle.

Line one or two oven trays with baking paper, depending on their size, and draw 3 circles on the paper of approximately 20cm in diameter. Preheat the oven to 180°C (350°F).

Over a medium heat, lightly toast the finely ground hazelnuts in a dry pan for 2 minutes then place in a glass bowl to cool. When cool, add the cornflour and 75g (3oz) of the caster sugar.

Whisk the egg whites and cream of tartar until they form soft peaks. Lower the speed on the mixer and gradually add the remaining caster sugar, then the vinegar and vanilla essence and beat until it forms stiff peaks. Fold the hazelnut mixture into the egg whites, mix well and spoon into the piping bag. Pipe 3 flat circles within the lines drawn on the paper, starting from the outside and moving inwards in a circular motion. Sprinkle half the crushed hazelnuts onto one of the rounds and bake in the oven for 30 minutes. If preparing in advance allow to cool and store in an airtight con-tainer for up to 36 hours.

Bring the cream to the boil in a saucepan then remove it from the heat and stir in the chocolate until it has melted. Add the brandy and the remaining hazelnuts and stir well.

Take one of the plain meringue discs (without the crushed hazelnuts) and spread it with half of the chocolate cream. Place the second plain disc over this and spread with almost all of the remainder of the cream, reserving 4 tablespoons. Top with the last remaining disc, hazelnuts facing upwards, and spread the remaining chocolate cream around the sides of the cake. (You may need to heat it slightly to make it a little more malleable.) Before serving, sprinkle the cake with icing sugar.

Marrons Glacés

You can buy marrons glacés from any good deli. Basically they are candied chestnuts; they sound horrible but they actually taste delicious and are terribly festive. (They were quite the rage in the Forties and Fifties.) Simply arrange the glacés decoratively on a plate and serve as you would petits fours.

We had a magical evening. It was one the best New Year's Eves I have ever had. I was Sophia Loren for the evening, he was Peter Sellers from the movie *The Millionairess* and, yes, and we did the song, 'Goodness Gracious Me!'

Our guests for the evening were:

Marilyn Monroe in *How to Marry a Millionaire*
Clark Gable as Rhett Butler from *Gone With the Wind*
Alfred Hitchcock as himself
Lauren Bacall in *To Have and Have Not*
John Wayne on a horse (don't ask)

Bette Davis in *All About Eve*
Elizabeth Taylor and Richard Burton in *Cleopatra*
Grace Kelly in *High Society*
Humphrey Bogart in *Casablanca*

We had asked people to dress their characters in evening wear and, boy, did they! There were enough fake diamonds, marabou feathers and satin bows to clothe an army of drag queens.

Anyway, the point of the exercise was to stop the bickering and start having some fun again. You do it any way you choose; if it involves food so much the better – make pizza from scratch together, toast some crumpets, eat cheese on toast in bed watching your favourite movie – do whatever it takes to get a smile out of each other. Get happy and pull out all the stops because you're not going to like the alternative.

My ex and I had a wonderful time and did actually stop bickering for a while there. I would love to tell you that we lived happily ever after, however sometimes things just don't work out, but at least you know you tried.

THE END IS NIGH . . .

❦

. . . But Let's Pretend It's Not

*Love is great glue but there's no cement
like mutual hate.*

LOUISE WYE

Ouch, things still not going too well, huh? More bad days than good? Sex life non-existent? Watching more and more mindless TV and talking less and less? What can I tell you, you have some stormy weather coming your way but ultimately it is for the greater good, it just doesn't feel that way when you're in it. The beginning of The End comes when we realise, with heavy hearts, that we are in the midst of Romantic Love and not, as we dared hope, True Love.

There is a difference. A Big One.

The latter has at least a chance of lasting, whereas the former? Well, it might play itself out over a protracted period of time, in some cases years, but ultimately it is doomed to fail if the person in whose basket we so tenderly placed all of our eggs is not actually *The One*.

(This is going to take some pretty intense explaining. Do not stop reading now because you need to know for the next time, and there will be a next time. See The Beginning.)

The End occurs because Romantic Love, by definition, cannot sustain itself beyond a certain critical point. It fades, dies or is replaced by resignation in the form of a marriage born of defeat or habit, or in some cases by children and, in most cases, ultimately, by divorce. (That, my friend, is for another book.)

I know you don't want to hear it so I'll be gentle with you, let me put it this way: imagine, if you will, that the two of you are trees. (Indulge me.) You are planted next to each other in a beautiful meadow and over time and with lots of tender loving care you grow strong and healthy.

Now imagine yourselves in full bloom. Heavy with delicate pink blossoms, thousands of flowers adorning your branches, a gentle breeze caressing your perfectly-formed petals. You are beautiful, a joy to behold.

The problem with blossom is that it flowers fleetingly and is fragile in the extreme; an average spring shower can scatter the petals far and wide, banishing all the pretty flowers to the ground.

Blossom is akin to the first flush of Romantic Love; beautiful, captivating, but short-lived.

In the book *Captain Corelli's Mandolin* the author, Louis de Bernières, refers to this very analogy and goes on to say that True Love exists when all the pretty blossom has fallen from the tree. At that juncture we find that our respective roots have become so entwined that we are now one. Warts an' all. That, my friend, is *True Love*.

I think our Louis has a point!

> *If the sun and moon should doubt*
> *they'd immediately go out.*
>
> WILLIAM BLAKE

We agreed at The Beginning that True Love is elusive and you've gotta kiss a lot of toads before you find your prince.

The sad thing is that whilst our *amour du jour* may not be *The One*, it's probably taken a while to figure it all out and in the interim we have invested an awful lot of time and energy in what, as it transpires, is essentially a 'doppelganger' relationship. Close, but no cigar!

It sort of felt like love, sometimes it even tasted like love, but now you've ended up with more cons than pros and it's just not fun anymore. And you're not sure it ever will be again.

I'm not suggesting that every relationship you will ever have is doomed and will end in tears, but please remember that we are seeking the Holy Grail, *The One*. We're not talking about second best here.

Whilst my cynicism knows no bounds I do believe that there is someone out there for everyone and, one day, with a little patience and a lot of effort, we will meet them.

It is surely a matter of principle not to settle for anything but the best, and a principle is not a principle until it costs us something.

Love is an endless act of forgiveness.

ANON

However, can you forgive? More to the point, do you want to? Even if you did, could you forget? And, frankly, can you be bothered?

Time to deal with the nuts and bolts of The End. What really happens when the petals fall from the trees and your roots can't stand the sight of each other, in fact they are not so much entwining as actively retreating.

What actually occurs to suggest that perhaps this is not *The One*? Why do we start picking fault, bickering and being less than charming towards each other? When does the constant desire to be anywhere *they are not* kick in? At which point did our bed go from being a place of unutterable joy to an extension of the battlefield?

Let's analyse this . . .

In The Beginning everything your new love says and does is terribly clever, very sweet, hysterically funny or mildly (fabulously) eccentric – depending on the situation.

When they talk, we listen with rapt attention; when they eat, we think that weird sucking noise they make is kinda sweet; when they leave the loo seat up (again!), we smile indulgently, happy to put it down, loving that they are in our space. What's a stray loo seat between new lovers? Things are going *so* well. The sex is fabulous. We can handle a few cute little idiosyncrasies, can't we?

When The End is nigh and love starts to lose its shine all these little things start to irk us. The stuff that is most endearing at The Beginning is the stuff that irritates us most towards The End.

We all have our own examples of what was once endearing and eventually became bloody irritating: baby voices, socks on the floor, knickers on the radiator, pet names (!), inability to perform simple tasks (putting the loo seat down), their god-awful friends and demanding families . . . once we were beside ourselves with excitement at the thought of meeting the people closest to our new love, now when they 'pop in' we head out the back door with great gnashing of teeth and a few choice words.

Any of this familiar?

I know, all this sounds harsh but just as you can't stop

yourself from falling into Romantic Love, it's impossible to stop from falling out of it.

As we have already ascertained, you cannot un-know what you know. You can, perhaps, lie to each other but you cannot lie to yourself. Scarily, some people choose this stage to commit to each other, hoping a big white wedding, a shed-load of presents and an exotic honeymoon will fix things. *Newsflash!* It won't.

Now it is just a matter of time, a few screaming matches or resolute silence (depending on the kind of people you are), before someone moves out and you both move on.

There is, of course, a period of transition, a time of let's try agains which are driven by fading memories of good times as we hold tightly to the past, while watching the present crumble round us. We both know there really is no future.

'Time for a little something.'

A. A. MILNE'S WINNIE THE POOH

Food (thank God we're back to food) at this point becomes a source of comfort, an olive branch, the catalyst that can still bind us, even if only briefly. We can still enjoy the pleasure of eating together. It is also a great sex substitute. (Let's be frank here, if you were shagging like bunnies we would still be in The Middle.)

The first thing that goes is the sex. C'mon, you know it

and I know it, but when you both know it, it's tragic. Back to food, please.

Towards The End we pretty much stop entertaining per se. We invite closerthanthis girlfriends for comfort food and wine-fuelled sessions of endless discussions about 'what went wrong'. Conversely, he invites the boys over to watch the footie and the parents get the odd invite to Sunday lunch. (Which is now strictly one course and bought ice-cream.) The 'terribly civilised' sparkling suppers for our very clever and oh-so-trendy friends and acquaintances that once consisted of four courses, an amuse-bouche and a palate-cleansing sorbet, are also just a distant memory.

What we want now is good solid food: plainish but not boring fare that can be easily prepared and can be eaten whilst watching telly (thus avoiding making conversation) and preferably with just a fork.

Here are a couple of my favourite supper dishes for those truly awful days when you need culinary Valium to feed you both and to help pour oil on troubled waters.

Toad in the Hole

This combination of hot sticky sausages, light as a feather pudding and steaming onion gravy puts a smile on my face even when I don't feel I have too much to smile about. It's almost impossible to stay sad or mad when someone cooks Toad.

150g (5oz) plain flour; 2 eggs, lightly beaten; 150ml (5fl oz)
milk; 100ml (3½fl oz) water; 6–8 good-quality sausages; salt
and freshly ground black pepper.
Gravy: 1 large Spanish onion; 1 tsp fresh thyme; 1 tbsp butter; 1 Kallo chicken stock cube, mixed with 400ml (14fl oz)
boiling water; 1 tsp cornflour; salt and freshly ground pepper.

Preheat the oven to 200°C (400°F). Sift the flour into a
mixing bowl, make a well in the centre, pour in the eggs
and beat together, gradually adding the flour, milk, water
and seasoning. (I use a hand whisk but an electric one will
do the job twice as fast.) Leave it to stand in a warm place
whilst you put the sausages into a large square metal tin
and put them in the oven for 20 minutes.

Meanwhile, make the gravy. Slice the onion into very
fine rings, heat the butter in a heavy-bottomed pan, add
the onion, sugar and seasoning and cook until very soft.
Add the stock and the cornflour, mixed with a little hot
water to form a paste, and simmer gently for 20 minutes.

After 20 minutes remove the sausages from the oven
and immediately pour over the batter. Put the whole thing
back in the oven for a further 25 minutes until the
Yorkshire pudding is crisp and golden.

Serve yourself a big slice of pudding smothered in onion
gravy – I promise that you will instantly feel a helluva lot
better.

Pasta e Fagioli

A rich Tuscan soup that is supper in a bowl: simple, healthy and very, very comforting.

225g (8oz) dried Borlotti beans soaked overnight in cold water (or use tinned if you're pushed for time); 1 onion, finely chopped; 50ml (2fl oz) extra virgin olive oil; 2 garlic cloves, crushed and finely chopped; 1 litre chicken stock (preferably homemade but you can cheat and use Kallo chicken organic stock cubes); 400g (14oz) tinned tomatoes, chopped; 150g (5oz) conchigliette (small pasta shells); freshly ground salt and pepper; 1 large handful of grated Parmesan.

Heat the olive oil in a large, heavy-bottomed saucepan, add the onion and garlic and cook over a gentle heat until soft. Add the drained beans and stock, cover and gently simmer for an hour and then add the tomatoes and continue to simmer for another hour.

Remove about half the beans and mash them thoroughly. Return them to the soup along with the pasta and cook for a further 15 minutes until the pasta is very tender. (You really don't want it al dente for this dish, it needs to be soft.) Serve in the pot and at the last minute add an extra swirl of olive oil and the Parmesan.

Salt Cod Brandade with Leeks and Fried Eggs

Despite being very popular in Italy, until I went to Australia I had never really tried baccalà (salt cod). What a revelation! Its rather dull and unappetising name totally belies its creamy, luscious, ambrosial flavour, I cannot recommend it highly enough.

You have to start soaking the fish the night before but that's no great hardship, just bung it in some cold water and try to change it at least three times over the course of 24 hours.

500g (1lb 2oz) salt cod, buy from Italian or Greek delis; 1 clove garlic; 3 leeks; 3 potatoes; 4 tbsp butter; 1 tbsp olive oil; 4 tbsp double cream; 2 eggs; nutmeg; freshly ground salt and pepper; a handful of finely chopped, flat leaf parsley.

Place the drained and washed cod in a large pan full of cold water and bring to the boil with the whole clove of garlic. Let it simmer gently for 20 minutes, then drain. Reserve the cooking liquid, discarding the garlic clove. Using your fingers, peel the skin off the fish, remove all the bones then shred into small pieces.

Chop the leeks very finely, first lengthwise and then across, to form very fine dice. Peel the potatoes and cut into 1cm slices, then into tiny cubes. Melt half the butter in a frying pan, add the olive oil and cook the leeks gently for 10 minutes until soft. Add the potatoes and 500ml (15fl oz) of the cooking liquid and cook gently for 20 minutes until the potatoes are very soft. Mash the potatoes and leeks in the pan with a potato masher, adding a tablespoon of butter.

Add the flaked fish, cream, black pepper and parsley, a scant grating of nutmeg and heat through.

I like my salt cod served in a shallow soup bowl topped with a fried egg that has been cooked in butter, and a side order of hot toast. I'm convinced this is what angels eat when they have had a bad day.

ONCE MORE WITH FEELING . . .

৺

Toto, We're Not in Kansas Anymore

Honey, I'm going to miss you so much and it's
not just the sex, it's the food preparation too.

HOMER SIMPSON

Things seem to be going from bad to worse; you have finally had *that* conversation, the one you have both been avoiding for so long. Tragically, you both agree that unless things get better very soon (indeed, a whole lot better), drastic measures will have to be taken. Neither of you really wants that; you both want it to work but the feelings are gone, and suddenly all those ludicrous love songs about finding love and losing love are ringing horribly true.

Except, you want to avoid the unavoidable so you decide to make one last bid to recapture 'the feeling'. That means going back to The Beginning; back into Seduction Mode and surprising him by getting all dressed up in that little black dress he loves so much and which reminds you both of happier times. It's time to dig out those strappy black shoes with the impossibly high heels that drive him crazy, plus the black lacy Agent Provocateur lingerie that he gave you last Christmas but somehow you have never got round to removing from its glossy pink box.

You set about preparing a gorgeous dinner, you light some candles, play some soft music and try desperately to evoke the ghost of Lola.

It has to be worth a try.

Steamed Asparagus with Hollandaise Sauce

Seared Duck Breast with a Sour Cherry Sauce, Garlic Potatoes and Mixed Leaves

Roasted Sugared Peaches with Brandy, Maple Syrup and Butter

Due to the wonders of vacuum-fresh imported fruits and vegetables, we can now enjoy asparagus all year round. It needs nothing more than a careful hand and the lightest of sauces, such as a hollandaise. It is also fantastic served with some of your favourite cheese melted in a bowl over a pan of boiling water: think Gorgonzola, blue Brie, Taleggio, even good old Philadelphia, indeed, anything you fancy that will melt. Or you can simply serve your precious sexy little stems with melted butter. The dipping, sucking and licking factor of asparagus ensures it rates highly on the food-pornography meter, especially when you feed those saucy little spears to each other.

Ready-made hollandaise is perfectly acceptable if you must, but there is nothing quite like the taste or the satisfaction of homemade sauce. Go on, have a go. If you are worried about having a hollandaise-disaster, have some bought stuff handy just in case.

Steamed Asparagus with Hollandaise Sauce

500g (1lb 2oz) asparagus (it should be plump and green, avoid slightly white and woody spears); 175g (6oz) of butter; 1 tbsp wine vinegar; 2 tbsp lemon juice; 3 large egg yolks; a pinch of salt.

Melt the butter slowly in a saucepan. Place the wine vinegar and lemon juice in another saucepan and bring to the boil. Blend the egg yolks and salt in a liquidiser then, with the motor running, gradually add the hot lemon juice and vinegar. Do this very slowly to avoid separation, then add the melted butter equally slowly (with the motor running all the time), until the sauce has thickened. To keep it warm, place the finished sauce in a bowl over a pan of boiling water until ready to serve.

To steam the asparagus, cut off the woody end until all

you can see is the green centre of the stem. Place the asparagus in a colander or Chinese steamer basket over a pot of fast-boiling water and cook for 8 to 12 minutes, or until tender. (The timing depends on the thickness of the stems. Be careful not to overcook it as you don't want to end up with floppy, limp asparagus. Keep testing it until it is tender, but still retains some bite.)

Serve immediately on a warmed platter placed between you in the centre of the table with a bowl of warm hollandaise, lots of crusty bread – and don't forget the finger bowls.

Asparagus is designed to be eaten with one's fingers, not a knife and fork, it physically pains me to watch people in restaurants cut each glorious green stem into little pieces. One dunks, sucks then bites, there really is no other way.

Seared Duck Breast with a Sour Cherry Sauce

2 duck breasts around 200g (7oz) each; 250g (9oz) of good-quality Morello cherry jam, made with whole cherries; a large knob of unsalted butter; 250ml (8fl oz) good red wine; a bay leaf; sea salt and freshly ground black pepper.

Combine the cherry jam, the red wine, the bay leaf and a couple of good grinds of pepper and sea salt in a saucepan. Simmer gently over a medium heat for 30 minutes until the sauce has the consistency of thin cream. (If it gets too thick, add a little water.) Turn off the heat and beat in the butter to give it a lovely glossy sheen. This sauce can be made in advance and keeps well in a sterilised, sealed jar in the fridge.

Preheat the oven to 220°C (425°F). To ensure the duck breasts are dry, pat with kitchen paper and leave uncovered in a cool place for 2 hours before cooking. Slash the skin diagonally at about 1cm intervals and brush with a thin coating of the cherry sauce. Arrange on a rack over a baking tray skin-side up and roast for about 20 minutes; the skin should be crisp and the meat slightly pink. Once out of the oven, allow the meat to rest for 5 minutes and then slice on the diagonal into thin 1cm slices and serve fanned out on a bed of garlic potatoes. Serve the sauce separately and spoon generously over the meat. (Make sure the sauce is piping hot.) Serve with 2 handfuls of watercress and 2 handfuls of rocket mixed with a splash of the cherry sauce and a splash of olive oil.

Garlic Potatoes

500g (1lb 2oz) new potatoes; 4 tbsp olive oil; 2 cloves finely chopped garlic; a handful of finely chopped fresh parsley; sea salt and freshly ground black pepper.

Preheat the oven to 200°C (400°F). Chop the potatoes into 1in dice, place in a plastic bag with olive oil, garlic, salt and pepper. Shake well and tip the whole lot into a roasting tray and place in the oven for about 30 minutes or until brown and crisp. Finish with freshly chopped parsley and season to taste.

Roasted Sugared Peaches with Brandy

2 large fresh ripe peaches (white ones if you can get them); 2 tbsp of good-quality maple syrup; 8 very small knobs of butter; 2 tbsp of muscovado sugar; a shot glass of brandy.

This can be popped into the oven whilst you are enjoying the duck, as it cooks it smells just divine.

Preheat the oven to 200°C (400°F). Cut the peaches in half, split them to remove the stone and then place them cut-side up so that they fit snugly into a buttered oven-proof dish. Place a knob of butter and a teaspoon of sugar into each cavity. Combine the brandy and the maple syrup and pour over the peaches. Sprinkle with 1 tablespoon of sugar then dot with the remaining butter. Bake for around 20 minutes. These are exceptionally good served on their own or with good-quality vanilla bean ice-cream.

THE LAST DANCE . . .

How to Say Goodbye

> *Love knows not its own depth*
> *until the hour of separation*
>
> KAHLIL GIBRAN

After months, or maybe even years, of recriminations, tears and anger it would seem that this relationship has reached its conclusion.

It's over.

The time has finally come for you to somehow move on and the sad thing is that you both know it. You have given it your best shot and it's just not working. It really doesn't matter whose fault it is anymore, or who said what to whom and when, it's just very sad and somehow you have to sort out the practicalities and say goodbye.

No one meant for this to happen, you were both so sure of what you thought you were sure of. There's nothing left to say and nothing left to fight about. One of you stays in the home that you once shared and the other moves out. Right now it's just all too raw and you both need a little space and time to think.

The decision to move out is never an easy one. My abiding memory of the worst break-up of my life involved a protracted and painful conversation sat on the steps of a spiral staircase in the house we once called home. We talked, laughed and cried all night and in the morning we both knew with unwavering certainty that we had given it our best shot and there was nothing left for us to do but say goodbye. To quote Carrie in *Sex and the City*: 'We were so Over we needed a new word for Over.'

FOOD GLORIOUS FOOD

Filling the Void

He who eats alone, chokes alone.

ARAB PROVERB

For goodness sake, let's think about something else. Food is now a means of comfort. Despite the fact that there will be days when you simply can't eat at all, there will also be others where you seek solace in the kitchen. I am not suggesting for one moment that you take refuge in eating and end up gaining 20lbs in a bid to heal your broken heart, but sometimes finding a little comfort in food can help you get through those initial long, lonely evenings as the very fabric of your life changes and you learn to be alone again. Cooking is a great substitute for weeping, moping and a little too much reflection.

The food we crave when we are pining is sensible fare, not the exotic, sensual dinners of the past. Think Delia, not Ducasse. There'll be no more oysters and champagne here, but there will be shepherd's pie and chardonnay.

In dealing with The End I am neither going to propose nor expect you to prepare perfect menus to cope with the tragic demise of your relationship. Frankly, it would be inappropriate and you're probably too sad to bother anyway. What we need here is food that is relatively simple to prepare but delectable enough to make you feel a trifle spoilt, a touch cosseted and perhaps just a little bit better.

Comfort food doesn't occur through the text of a recipe, it's born of instinct; the need to fill an emotional void and, of course, hunger, but perhaps with a touch of compensatory, self-indulgent greed.

If you are anything like me, when I feel unhappy I head for the fridge. Sadly, I also do the same thing when I'm happy. I'm passionate about food and being miserable is just one of the myriad of excuses I use to indulge myself.

In the same vein as the delicious and easily-prepared post-coital 4am suppers of The Beginning, here are a few suggestions for comfort foods. These recipes should get you through those awful days in the closing stages of your liaison when you know it's over and you're in the midst of that mourning period which every failed relationship delivers in its wake.

This is the food for when you need a big, fat cuddle

from the one person that currently is least likely to oblige: the guy you're in the throes of breaking up with.

I know you're feeling lonely and there's a humungous black cloud over your head but, honey, a girl's gotta eat.

When asked, most people have very clear ideas about their preferred comfort foods. I've got lots of different suggestions but the numero uno, head honcho, big daddy of all comfort foods, without exception, has to be the humble mashed potato. Akin to a cuddle, and twice as soothing, it would seem mash and the end of a relationship go hand in hand in much the same way as strawberries and cream.

Perfect Mashed Potato

To produce heavenly clouds of perfect, fluffy mash boil some King Edward potatoes in plenty of salted water with their skins still on, until they are tender. Drain them and allow to cool. When they have cooled slightly, peel them. (They may be a little hot to the touch but in this case a little pain is a good thing and the bonus is that it will take your mind off the pain in your heart.) Mash the peeled, still-warm spuds with spectacularly large volumes of butter and cream, season with freshly ground salt and pepper and serve immediately. Reheated mash is like lukewarm love; cheerless, stodgy and somewhat limp.

(Some people make reference to the word 'shovelling in' when describing eating mashed potato, but I think it's a miserable word indeed when related to the consumption of something so gorgeous. If made with care the lowly mashed potato can be scrumptious and shovelling it in, rather than savouring it, would be a sin.)

For many of you, Comfort Food equals Takeaway Food: Chinese, Indian, Pizza, Fish and Chips, Pies and Burgers, and for the really hardened takeaway aficionado, Mexican. (Which in my humble opinion often looks like food that has already been digested then recycled but, hey, each to their own.) It would appear that people find comfort in just about anything that can be ordered by phone and delivered to the door in under 45 minutes. The attraction is twofold; firstly, the lack of any actual cooking or washing-up and secondly, the gratifying consolation of all those rather yummy soporific and satisfying calories.

Once again, as with post-coital suppers, most of the people I surveyed hankered for a steaming bowl of pasta. This time round, however, you wanted it served with a luscious sauce either made from fresh cream with mushrooms sautéed in butter or lots of different cheeses: from good old cheddar to the stronger ones such as Gorgonzola or Stilton. Some more simple souls, on the other hand, preferred linguine dressed with fresh sage leaves that had been sautéed in an obscene amount of butter and then doused with fresh Parmesan. Unsurprisingly, everyone loved the idea of oven-baked pasta, so here's a bit of cheat's version for solo dining.

Pasta with Meatballs

The meatballs: 150g (5oz) minced beef; 75g (3oz) sausage meat; thyme; freshly ground salt and pepper; 1 glass of red wine.

The béchamel sauce: 450ml (15fl oz) milk; 1 bay leaf; 4 peppercorns; 40g (1½oz) butter; 30g (1oz) plain flour.

300g (11oz) penne pasta; 1 jar of good-quality, ready-made, tomato-based pasta sauce.

Make up some little meatballs about the size of large gob-stoppers by combining all the ingredients. Fry the balls in a little olive oil until lightly browned and set aside. Deglaze the pan with a glass of red wine over a high heat and allow the alcohol to reduce by half.

Prepare the béchamel sauce by bringing the milk to the boil with the bay leaf and the peppercorns. Melt the butter in a separate saucepan and stir in the plain flour until it forms a roux. Add the milk bit by bit until it has all been incorporated and the sauce is smooth and glossy. Add a grating of nutmeg and season as required.

Cook the pasta in plenty of boiling water for 10 minutes, drain, then combine with a good-quality, ready-made, tomato-based pasta sauce (the cheating bit) and the wine-infused pan juices. Give it all a good stir and tip the whole thing into a well-buttered, glass, ovenproof dish.

Scatter the meatballs over the pasta and drown the whole lot in the béchamel sauce, top with freshly-grated Parmesan and bake in the oven at 180°C (350°F) for around 30 minutes until it's bubbling and golden.

Eat it piping hot with just a fork and a glass of red wine whilst watching your favourite soap on the telly, it's guaranteed to make you feel just that little bit more loved.

Nursery food came up a lot in my study: fish finger sandwiches, beans on toast, tinned macaroni cheese, chipolata sausages on sticks with ketchup for dipping, scrambled eggs, those chocolate or treacle puddings that you steam in their tins served with custard, and lots and lots of toast made with factory-produced pappy, thick-sliced white bread and lashings of unsalted butter. I love toast; my grandmother was a great believer that a slice of hot buttered toast with strawberry jam and scalding sweet tea was a cure for all ills.

My fondness for creating decadently delicious snacks developed early (at around seven or eight years old), and on the few precious occasions when I was left to my own devices in the kitchen I would experiment. And so it was that my Crunchy Pancake Toast was born: grill one side of a slice of white bread, liberally butter the other side and sprinkle with a generous amount of sugar and a good squeeze of lemon. Pop it back under the grill until the sugar turns golden brown. My friends, I give you Toast nirvana.

The only drawback to this recipe was that every time I made it I burnt my fingers! Honestly, you have to try this, it is le dernier cri in fabulous but oh-so-trashy food. It's a bit like lemon pancakes, but it's squidgier on the inside with a gorgeous lemon sharp, sugary crunch on the outside.

Those of you who were craving nursery food also wanted peanut butter and jam sandwiches, jelly and ice-cream, Marmite soldiers and chicken nuggets and chips – both cooked from frozen and served with peas. (Frozen, of course.)

Other friends that I asked also wanted a variety of convenience foods to pop in the oven or zap in a microwave on those days when cooking just simply isn't an option. There was mention of ready-made lasagne and cannelloni, as well as other Italian dishes such as ravioli and gnocchi.

There were also those who craved hearty stews made with beef and dumplings, or chicken casseroles, or pies (especially the tinned variety with suet crust pastry). Frozen chips were another winner, especially when served with lots of salt and vinegar. Also requested were those supermarket-brand Indian and Chinese meals where you get 5 or 6 different dishes in a special carrier bag for you to take home and reheat. Who says they're not meant to be a meal for just one?

Alarmingly, some of you like to soothe your flagging spirits and wounded hearts with those truly tragic TV dinners that come in compartmentalised white plastic trays. You know the ones, the meals that contain lumps of reconstituted chicken in a turgid sauce of cream and mushrooms, alongside the truly sad combination that is sweetcorn mixed with peas and all set off with a big lump of grey stodge that is supposedly mashed potato. The worst thing about TV dinners is that not only is the food inedible but, to add insult to injury, the trays buckle and start to disintegrate when heated so that one's entire meal tastes of melting plastic. Nasty! I don't want to nag and I know you're feeling blue, but if you must eat this stuff at least remove it from the packaging when you heat it up.

One of my favourite responses to the question 'what's your favourite comfort food' was the simple request for a never-ending bottle of white wine and 20 Marlboro Lights. Simple, but effective.

Happily, the hardened foodies amongst us wanted to cook properly; to lovingly prepare food for themselves just as they did when they were a 'we' instead of an 'I'. Perhaps not every night, but every now and then and especially at weekends when they found themselves home alone and needed the distraction and bittersweet solace of preparing and eating a wonderful meal.

My absolute favourite thing when I am in need of solace is that most sublime of Italian peasant food, risotto. The fact that it completely galvanises your attention for the 20 minutes it takes to prepare (thus distracting you from your woes) is a wonderfully cathartic bonus. I find myself almost hypnotised by the constant stirring necessary to ensure that the little grains of arborio rice swell and soften to form this ambrosial feast that cannot help but soothe. The following recipe for Risi e Bisi is somewhere between a risotto and a soup.

Risi e Bisi

200g (7oz) arborio rice; 150g (5oz) butter; 1 tsp olive oil; 1 litre (1¾ pints) of simmering chicken or vegetable stock (better fresh but a stock cube will do); 5 tbsp grated Parmesan cheese; 200g (7oz) cooked peas (frozen will do);1 small onion; 140ml (5fl oz) of white wine; freshly ground salt and pepper.

In a heavy-bottomed saucepan sweat the finely chopped onion in half the butter over a gentle heat for about 5 minutes, or until it is soft and translucent. Tip in the rice and stir. Pour in the wine and let it bubble for about 5 minutes then slowly start to add the hot stock, ladle by ladle, stirring constantly. As the stock is absorbed the rice will cook and swell and after about 10 minutes stir in the warmed peas and taste for seasoning. Continue to add stock and stir until the rice is cooked.

After about 20 minutes add the rest of the butter and 4 tablespoons of the cheese. The risotto should have the consistency of porridge, but if it appears a little dry stir in a final ladle of stock and serve immediately in soup plates. Top with the rest of the cheese and serve with a crisp white wine and perhaps a little salad. Heaven.

Roast chicken was another dish that topped the comfort-food poll. I find this is best prepared using a good free-range bird seasoned with plenty of rock salt and freshly ground pepper, anointed with butter (not only on top of the bird but also pushed under the skin of the breast), with half a lemon and several cloves of garlic stuffed into the body cavity.

Garlic Roast Chicken

Roast the bird in a hot oven for 20 minutes per 500g (1lb 2oz) and add on another 20 minutes. Allow the cooked chicken to rest for 10 minutes before carving. Eat with a watercress salad drizzled with olive oil and a splash of the juices from the pan with perhaps a side order of mashed potatoes. Make the gravy by reducing the remainder of the juices with a little white wine.

I suggest that if you do go to all this trouble you set the table with your nicest crockery, crack open a decent bottle of wine and eat your fill. Leftover chicken is a pleasure to have in the fridge and can be used in a million different ways, so don't worry about the extravagance.

You're worth it.

This is a recipe from a girlfriend of mine who seems to be constantly lurching from one emotional crisis to another; she's always either in love or in the depths of despair. Personally, I think she's hooked on this little tart but her obsession with staying thin means she only allows herself to eat it when she's feeling down.

Goat's Cheese, Caramelised Onion, Tomato and Anchovy Tart

(Serves 2)

1 red onion, finely sliced; 1 clove garlic, crushed and chopped; 1 tbsp butter; 1 tbsp olive oil; 2 tsp sugar; 1 pack frozen puff pastry, ready-rolled; 1 log of goat's cheese; 10 cherry tomatoes; 5 anchovies, drained and ripped into little pieces.

Heat the oven to 200°C (400°F). Melt the butter and olive oil in a heavy-bottomed saucepan and add the onions and garlic. Cook over a low heat until soft then add the sugar and cook for a further 5 minutes, stirring all the time so that the sugar doesn't catch. Set aside to cool. Slice the goat's cheese into thin-ish rounds and keep cool. Butter a baking tray, line it with the pastry and top this with a layer of caramelised onions and evenly-spaced discs of goat's cheese. Scatter the whole thing with small cherry tomatoes and the anchovies and bake in a hot oven for around 20–25 minutes until the cheese is melted and the pastry is golden. Serve immediately.

THE END

What do you reckon came after mashed potato as our most favourite comfort food? Chocolate, of course, lots and lots of it in lots of different ways: bars, buttons, nay bricks of it if we could but get our hands on it. The chocoholic is alive and well.

It is mooted in certain circles that chocolate is a great sex substitute, or is it the other way round? Is sex really just a substitute for chocolate?

We also want desserts: sticky toffee pudding, banoffee pie, apple pie, American pancakes with maple syrup, fresh strawberries served on toast with lots of cream cheese and sugar, as well as pints and pints of ice-cream and rivers of custard served with crumbles made from rhubarb or apricots. We also want mousses and caramels and gingerbread, all homemade on a rainy Sunday afternoon when we really don't know what else to do with ourselves.

It would seem that when we are sad our sweet tooth comes out to play and keeps us company. It would seem that misery keeps calorific company.

As for my own personal preference, when I was feeling particularly low one night and was in full-on, fridge-monster mode, I wanted a taste from my childhood that I could eat in bed whilst reading and was guaranteed to help me sleep. I had some cooked rice in the fridge to which I added a small tin of coconut cream and a chopped banana. I gently heated all of this together until it bubbled then poured it all into a deep soup bowl and sprinkled it with brown sugar. It tasted divine, as well as having an incredibly soporific and soothing effect akin to sinking into a big feather mattress.

Another tried and tested favourite is to place squares of sponge cake in a cereal bowl (the squares of trifle sponges you can buy work really well), cover them with hot milk and sprinkle with cinnamon and muscovado sugar. It feels like you have swallowed a hot water bottle but, never having eaten a hot water bottle, I presume it tastes much nicer.

THE SIX STAGES
OF THE END

How To Mend a Broken Heart

You can always tell when a relationship is over, little things start grating on your nerves, 'would you please stop that! That breathing in and out is so repetitious.'

ELLEN DEGENERES

Let us take a moment to reflect, recap and make sure we recognise and understand the various stages that make up The End.

1. The Seminal Moment

The Seminal Moment in the demise of a relationship is easily defined. It's that split second when you look at the person you once loved and realize with devastating lucidity that you just don't feel the same way anymore, and probably never will again.

Many of us try to pretend that the heart-stopping sub-conscious moment of painful discovery didn't really happen and we kid ourselves that everything is going to be ok but, I repeat, you can't un-know what you know.

That shocking, ruinous flash of reality can happen months or sometimes even years before the actual break-up occurs. Everybody has a different story to tell about the moment when they knew in their hearts it was over. In some cases it happened seemingly over something and nothing – a glance or a throwaway remark, whereas in others it was far more dramatic – a betrayal that on the surface we tried hard to forgive but which, ultimately, proved in our hearts to be unforgivable.

At this early stage of a break-up, whilst we are both painfully aware of the problem we are inclined to ignore it and soldier on, choosing not to discuss it in the hope that it will go away and we can go back to where we were and be happy again.

During this stage you both strive to avoid situations where the two of you are alone and where there might be even the slightest possibility of a D&M (deep and mean-ingful conversation). Intimate dinners are no longer an option, you tend to surround yourselves with friends when dining out, and the dinners you share at home which were once intimate suppers à deux have become a ménage à trois – you, him and the television – as every meal is eaten in front of the box in a bid to avoid conversation and thereby any contentious issues.

2. Separate Lives

The tacit agreement *not* to deal with the issues behind the ever-widening gulf between you continues into the next phase of The End.

You start spending more and more time apart. It appears fairly innocuous to start with; going to bed at separate times, going for a quick drink after work rather than going home, finding a new hobby that doesn't interest (and therefore doesn't involve) the other.

Mine was going to the gym. Having never been that keen on exercise I suddenly found myself in the health club seven days a week spending inordinately long periods of time working out. It could just be that I was hooked on the endorphins that come with excessive exercise but, realistically, the time-consuming and gruelling workouts stopped as soon as the relationship did. Go figure!

At this stage, whilst you both recognise there is a problem, neither of you choose to acknowledge it thus avoiding the truth and the moment of confrontation that you know *must* surely come.

Sadly, this is the stage where the principal enemy of love and reconciliation rears its ugly little head, that most capricious and fickle of emotions: indifference.

For while you are arguing and bickering it proves you still care enough to do so thereby affording you the possibility (no matter how slight) of rekindling what once was. When anger and hurt are replaced by apathy and ennui, however, it is tantamount to throwing a bucket of water over the last embers of the love you once shared.

Eating at this stage tends to be a rather solitary affair or, worse, elaborate dinners are prepared with trepidation as some kind of olive branch. Of course, these meals tend to idle in the oven awaiting the return of someone who is either late or not coming home at all, whereupon it ends up in the bin amid feelings of resentment at having bothered to cook at all.

3. Make Up to Break Up

Things have come to a head and you can't pretend any longer. The time has come to sit down and talk things through.

The realisation that things can't go on as they are even for one more day, can be triggered by the slightest thing. It happens when you reach the end of your tether, realising just how miserable you feel and how unhappy you are making yourself and your partner; who, deep down, you still care for even though it's hard to believe that right now.

Thus, you decide to have the conversation you have been avoiding for months. It's generally a good idea to do this on neutral ground as, ironically, in much the same vein as the first date dinner, you need to be able to just sit, talk and understand each other. Cooking dinner just gets in the way and, in all honesty, do you really want to?

Once you've had the conversation and understand each other's grievances it is easier to move forward and try to work things out. I'm not saying that all relationships are salvageable, but one should at least try.

4. Realisation

Realisation occurs in three stages once you have both accepted there is a problem and it is at last out in the open.

Stage 1

This stage is a period of one-more-chances and let's-try-agains as you strive to improve your clearly deteriorating relationship and give it one last shot whilst also mutually acknowledging and grudgingly accepting that it may not work out.

Thus you *make an effort* to stop going out separately and to start communicating again; which means discussing your relationship late into the night (sometimes ad nauseam) and trying desperately to recapture the sexual wonderland and Pink Cloud ecstasy of The Beginning.

Seduction dinners are once again on the menu; those candle lit evenings that are cooked together or that one of you prepared to surprise the other. These evenings might sometimes succeed but will more often fall short of expectations as unresolved issues come to the fore. Either way, they bring you a little closer together and make you feel you are at least trying.

Stage 2
You're back in denial once more; you're leading separate lives once again and the indifference is not only more obvious, but also a lot more painful.

One of the harsh realities of life is that one person is always more ready to walk away than the other. Therefore, one person is usually in denial and executing that most painful of relationship tools: avoidance.

At this stage you simply pretend it's not happening. You act as though everything is ok and the efforts you are making are having a positive effect on the demise of that which you hold so dear.

I'm not even going to mention food at this point. To the best of my recollection it was the only time in my life I stopped eating altogether, or if I did eat it was toast, biscuits and the odd fried egg sandwich. Meals together are now few and far between and are always eaten in front of the telly or with false cheerfulness, as you both desperately try to think of something to say that won't lead to another post-mortem of what went wrong.

Stage 3

Acceptance. That awful moment when, with heavy hearts, you both acknowledge that it's time for a little space and introspection. Reluctantly, you relinquish your now tenuous bond and wish each other well.

When it's harder to stay with somebody than it is to leave, it's time to say goodbye. Even though it's hard, you need to remember that without endings there can be no renewal and no new beginning.

OUCH . . . IT HURTS . . .

There is no end.
There is no beginning.
There is only the infinite passion of life.

FEDERICO FELLINI

Knowledge is power and for that reason please see this summary of the six phases of recovery from The End.

If you know what to expect it's so much easier to deal with. There is no fixed time for each phase, everyone is different, just trust that stage 6 *will* come because it will and you will learn from your pain and your mistakes.

1. Disbelief and Depression. (Feeling numb, getting used to living alone again. Going through the motions, existing, not living.)
2. Tears and Tantrums. (Calling them at all hours; shouting, sobbing, accusing, in fact wallowing in being a victim

and possibly even quite enjoying it. Your friends are getting sick of hearing about it.)
3. Melancholy Isolation. (Sad songs, sad movies, sad literature, never going out. Really bloody sad, actually.)
4. Anger and Indignation. (How dare he/she treat *me* like that? Anger is good, cleansing, cathartic. Go, baby, get mad.)
5. Bored With It. (Yawn. Enough angst already, you are even bored with yourself. The sex was fairly crap towards the end anyway.)
6. Eyes meet across a crowded room, at a party, on the tube, even at Grandma's funeral. *Kapow!* Here we go again . . .

The clouds will pass. The sun will shine and you will live to fight another day. And love again.

ALL YOU NEED IS LOVE . . .

ॐ

And Staying Power

Marriage is forever, it's like cement.

PETER O'TOOLE

So there you have it, the three stages of love as defined by *Eat Me*; ranging from the rapturous ecstasy of that very first glance to the anguished despair of the final farewell, alongside every other emotion in between.

There are those who, having read this book, may find my stance a touch cynical and perhaps feel I have little or no faith in the existence of true love and enduring passion.

They couldn't be more wrong.

Whilst to date I have certainly had my fair share of 'almost but not quite' relationships, I will confess to having exceptionally high standards when it comes to finding 'the one'. This is with very good reason, as I have before my very eyes a living example of what I think we should all be aiming for.

My parents have been married for 53 years; Mum was 16 when they met and 21 when they got married and, despite many ups and downs through the trials and tribulations that life throws at *all* of us, when the going got tough their relationship just got stronger and stronger, seemingly nurtured by the bad times almost as much as the good.

Yes, sure, they fought sometimes (Italian men and women are kind of designed that way), but they always ended up on the same side. The grass was never greener; breaking up was never an option.

Theirs is a story that should gladden our hearts and give us all a little faith in the power of true love, and indeed in the veracity of its very existence: two ordinary people who are far from perfect and yet who, after all these years, still love each other enough to want to spend all of their time together. (Going back to Louis de Bernières' theory, their roots are so entwined that they now form but a single tree.)

True Love is not about hearts and flowers, from what I can see it's about respect, loyalty, trust and endurance. That's what I want.

As we agreed earlier, a principle isn't a principle until it costs us something. Personally, I will keep paying my dues until I find 'the one' and I won't settle for anything or anyone less. Might I suggest you do the same.

I would like to end on a sweet note, with a recipe from my mother. These Boozy Cherries have comforted me through many a broken heart and I hope will do the same for you.

Cigliege Sotto Spirito – Boozy Cherries (or if you have had more than you should, Choosy Berries)

They need to infuse for at least 3 months before they are ready to eat, but they are well worth the wait.

1kg (2lb 4oz) cherries with stalks on; ½ litre (15fl oz) pure 95% alcohol; 400g (14oz) caster sugar; 200ml (7fl oz) dry white wine; 2 x 500g (1lb 2oz) jars with rubber seals.

Don't wash the cherries, simply wipe them clean with a soft dry cloth. Leave the stalks on but trim them so that they are quite short (this stops the cherries from bleeding during maceration). Bring the wine to the boil in a saucepan and dissolve the sugar thoroughly to form a syrup. Allow it to cool completely.

Place the dry, clean cherries into the two jars, 500g (1lb 2oz) in each, divide the sugar syrup between them and top with the alcohol. Place a disc of waxed paper over the top of each jar and seal.

Put the jars in a dry, cool dark cupboard and don't even think about opening them for at least 3 months – the longer you leave them the better they will be. We make them in June in time for Christmas.

To serve, place a few cherries in a glass with a little liquor and eat with a cocktail stick, I promise you that you have never had a taste explosion quite like it.

Maybe these cherries are one reason my parents have survived 53 years of marriage, after a few of these you're practically anaesthetised!

PLAYLIST:

Justin Timberlake: **Cry Me a River**
Sinead O'Connor: **Nothing Compares 2 U**
Harry Nillsson: **Without You**
Bill Withers: **Ain't No Sunshine**
Destiny's Child: **Survivor**
Alanis Morissette: **You Oughta Know**
Michael Jackson: **She's Out of My Life**
Aretha Franklin: **Respect**
Leonard Cohen: **I'm Your Man**
The Fugees: **Killing Me Softly**

POSTSCRIPT

POSTSCRIPT

So this is the end; but before we part do allow me to share with you a few of my personal great food memories that evoke in me a feeling of total pleasure and love:

The prawns and roasted Bresse chicken, followed by Crêpes Suzette, remain in my heart always, as it was my first.

A garlicky, tomato-based, heavenly fish soup I had in a beachside restaurant in Marseilles on an extended French sojourn with a very charming Frenchman. What can I tell you? I'm a sucker for a French accent.

A dozen snails in garlic butter followed by steak frites and salad eaten in a tiny French restaurant on Southgate Green many, many times with my first proper boyfriend.

Gnocchi cooked by my Auntie Vicky on New Year's Day several years ago when the entire family turned up and my brother ate 5 platefuls. They were perfect, and I haven't eaten gnocchi since as I know they just could not compare and even if they did, it wouldn't be the same without everybody there.

The banquet that took place yearly at my grandparents' farm followed the threshing of the wheat, where the whole family and many friends from neighbouring farms toiled for an entire day to get the job done in record time. When it was all over, my grandmother and all the other wives and daughters would prepare a magnificent feast, starting with antipasto and 10 different types of pasta. The main event was a myriad of roasted meats; whole suckling pigs, baby lambs, wild boar and roasted chicken, served with a mind-blowing array of vegetables, fresh from my grand- mother's garden and gallons of my grandfather's home- made wines, chilled from the cellar. The party would go on late into the night and everyone would join in the singing and dancing. Wonderful days.

Spicy Indian curries eaten on board my fiancé's parents' boat in Hong Kong on Sunday lunchtimes whilst sailing around the islands. Nothing tasted better, especially when it was preceded by a large Bloody Mary.

Two dozen oysters and a bottle of champagne shared with a very good friend at Bibendum restaurant over the course of one perfect summer.

An impromptu lunch on a splendidly sunny day by the beach, in the fairy-tale city of Barcelona, with Roger. We gorged ourselves on freshly caught chargrilled squid followed by baby lamb chops with tiny rosemary potatoes, broad beans steeped in cold-pressed olive oil, and homemade saffron bread, with far too much ridiculously cheap but seriously good local vino. It was the most romantic lunch I've ever had. *Il sole bacia I belli.* (The sun kisses only the beautiful.)

Every meal I have ever shared with my family. I know that sounds corny, but we are truly blessed as my mother is a fantastic cook and never seems to tire of it or us.

INDEX OF RECIPES